Rome
Houses

Rome Houses

teNeues

Editor in chief: Paco Asensio

Editor and texts: Cynthia Reschke

Editorial coordination: Haike Falkenberg

Art director: Mireia Casanovas Soley

Layout: Ignasi Gracia Blanco

English translation: Robert J. Nusbaum

French translation: Marion Westerhoff, Christine Belakhda

Spanish translation: Almudena Sasiain

Published by teNeues Publishing Group

teNeues Publishing Company
16 West 22nd Street, New York, NY 10010, USA
Tel.: 001-212-627-9090, Fax: 001-212-627-9511

teNeues Book Division
Kaistraße 18
40221 Düsseldorf, Germany
Tel.: 0049-(0)211-994597-0, Fax: 0049-(0)211-994597-40

teNeues Publishing UK Ltd.
P. O. Box 402
West Byfleet
KT14 7ZF, Great Britain
Tel.: 0044-1932-403509, Fax: 0044-1932-403514

www.teneues.com

ISBN: 3-8238-4564-0

Editorial project: © 2003 LOFT Publications
Via Laietana, 32 4° Of. 92
08003 Barcelona, Spain
Tel.: 0034 932 688 088
Fax: 0034 932 687 073

e-mail: loft@loftpublications.com
www.loftpublications.com

Printed by: Gràfiques 94, St. Quirze del Vallès, Spain. March 2004

Bibliographic information published by Die Deutsche Bibliothek Die Deutsche Bibliothek lists this publication in the Deutsche Nationalbibliografie; detailed bibliographic data is available in the Internet at http://dnb.ddb.de.

Table of Contents
Inhalt   Indice   Sumario

Table of Contents

Inhalt   Indice   Sumario

Introduction

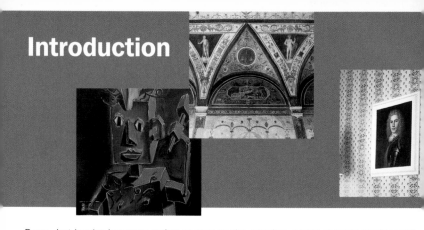

Rome. Just hearing her name makes us want to give ourselves over to pleasant musings and, perhaps, blissful memories. A city that fascinates like almost no other place on earth.

Rome. The lovely, eternal, open city. The city that has always elicited countless words of praise. For several millennia, she has been a backdrop for the ebb and flow of history, for pinnacles of cultural achievement, for art, ideas and untold dynamism. We think of stones in her regard. Ancient stones and a tangle of streets snaking up hills, narrow streets with people milling about— and titanic traffic. The fragrance of freshly brewed cappuccino creates a backdrop for a veritable parade of smartly dressed people, as well as the ubiquitous tourists in clotted groups or questing for culture by ones and twos. Or the striking silhouettes of Romans with their glossy hair and the sunglasses they wear—seemingly round the clock. The ambiance is colorful, turbulent, joyful ... punctuated by dramatic facial expressions and hand gestures. Film clips mingle with picture-postcard idylls, while illustrations from history books merge with memories of visits to museums and TV images of the Pope blessing the crowds in St. Peter's square.

There are so many churches and small, winding streets that the visitor can simply abscond from everyday reality—although in truth it's the renowned monuments that set our pulses racing. The Vatican and the dome of St. Peter's, the Coliseum, the Roman forum, the Mausoleum, the Spanish Steps, the Pantheon and the Fontana di Trevi—the latter a name you can savor on your tongue like creamy stracciatella ice cream, or utter ardently to the object of your affections à la Kevin Kline in "A Fish Called Wanda".

Intriguing shops, fashion boutiques, restaurants, bars and cafes—the list of distractions from museums and other cultural pleasures is long. But one thing is for sure: no one is ever bored in Rome. However, this book does not concern itself with the Eternal City's fabled past—to the contrary. In **Rome Houses**, you will not be looking at Rome through the window of a hotel or tour bus, but will instead tour some of Rome's most fascinating dwellings, where antique doors creak open, and rooftop gardens barely visible from the street below provoke a longing to while away

your time gazing at Rome's hills. Or where the sight of shiny chrome kitchen utensils makes you want to bargain for your daily groceries at Roman markets with their stalls abounding with an astonishing array of wonderful food.

Romans are profoundly affected by the omnipresent and inescapable beauty of their city. In private homes, villas and apartments, the visitor encounters an astonishing range of styles and atmospheres created by architects and interior designers—or even by the residents themselves. These decors radiate tremendous charm, blend harmoniously with their architectonics and are replete with art, antiques and collector's items. In the houses and apartments in this book, the old and new rub shoulders, designer furnishings create accents in spaces with clean lines, and the materials used bear testimony to the expertise and care that went into selecting them.

Some apartments have been adroitly converted into floor-through dwellings so as to create more living space, and dividing walls have been erected or removed to tailor the ground plan to the residents' needs. A desk with a computer on it fits neatly into a niche, while built-in closets provide sight line-friendly storage space. An old-fashioned open hearth fireplace may evoke memories of the social customs of yesteryear, while modern fireplaces can warm up the atmosphere of a room both emotionally and physically. Exposed beam ceilings provide a welcome contrast to the minimalism of predominantly white decors. Residents' groupings of collector's items and fine art that have been acquired over long periods arouse in us the desire to find out more about the residents and their lives. Each of the houses and apartments in this book is a haven of privacy—a retreat from the ubiquitous hurly-burly of Rome's streets and squares.

The publishers would like to express their gratitude to all those who invited us into their homes for a "behind the scenes" glimpse of their lives. We hope that by the time you read the last page of this book—if not sooner—you'll decide that on your next visit to Rome you'll throw coins into the Trevi fountain until you too can revel in the kind of homes described in **Rome Houses**.

Einleitung

Rom – es sind nur wenige Buchstaben und dennoch möchte man bei ihrem Klang augenblicklich in andächtiges Schweigen versinken und sich Tagträumen und eventuell verklärten Erinnerungen hingeben. Von dieser Stadt geht eine Faszination aus wie nur von wenigen Orten auf unserer Erde.

Rom – die schöne, die ewige, die offene Stadt ... Wie viele Adjektive kann sie auf sich vereinigen? Schauplatz über Jahrtausende für eine bewegende Geschichte, hohe Kultur, Kunstschätze, Einfallsreichtum, Dynamik. Steine tauchen vor dem inneren Auge auf, sehr alte Steine und ein Gewirr aus breiten, sich die Hügel hinaufwindenden Straßen und kleinen Gassen, Menschengewühl und atemberaubender Straßenverkehr. Der Duft von frisch gebrühtem Cappuccino bildet den Hintergrund für ein Defilee gut gekleideter Menschen, dazwischen allenthalben Touristen in Gruppen oder als wissensdurstige Einzelgänger. Markante römische Profile, glänzendes Haar und Sonnenbrillen zu jeder Tages- und Nachtzeit. Das Bild ist bunt und turbulent, lebensfroh und gestenreich. Filmausschnitte mischen sich mit Postkartenidyllen, Zeichnungen aus Geschichtsbüchern mit Erinnerungen an Museumsbesuche und aktuellen Fernsehbildern von der letzten Übertragung des päpstlichen Segens.

Ungezählt sind die Kirchen, Gassen und Winkel, der Besucher kann sich einfach vom belebten Alltag mitreißen lassen, doch sind es vor allem die weltweit berühmten Monumente, die unsere Herzen höher schlagen lassen: Der Vatikan mit dem Petersdom, das Kolosseum, das Forum Romanum, das Mausoleum, die Spanische Treppe, das Pantheon, um nur einige zu nennen, sowie – man mag den Namen auf der Zunge zergehen lassen wie ein cremiges Stracciatella-Eis oder mit der Inbrunst vortragen, mit der einst Kevin Kline in dem Film „Ein Fisch namens Wanda" sich und seine Partnerin in Stimmung bringen wollte – la Fontana di Trevi ...

Kuriose Geschäfte, Modeboutiquen, Restaurants, Bars, Cafés, die Ablenkung von den Museen und anderen Kunstschätzen ist groß – nur langweilen kann man sich in der Hauptstadt Italiens kaum. Doch geht es in diesem Buch einmal nicht um dieses bekannte Gesicht der Stadt, sondern ganz im Gegenteil – die Leser sollen statt aus dem Fenster des Hotelzimmers oder Touristenbusses in die privatesten Gemächer der heutigen Römer schauen. Alte Türen öffnen sich

mit einem Knarren, Dachgärten, von denen man von unten von der Straße aus nur eine leise Vorahnung bekommt, laden zum genüsslichen Verweilen über den sieben Hügeln ein und chromblitzende Küchenutensilien regen dazu an, auf den üppigen Märkten die tausenderlei Spezialitäten tatsächlich in haushaltsüblichen Mengen zu erhandeln.

Entziehen können sich die Römer der Schönheit ihrer Stadt nicht. In den privaten Villen, Häusern und Wohnungen begegnen dem Besucher die verschiedensten Stile und Atmosphären, entwickelt von Architekten, Innenarchitekten oder den designbewussten Bewohnern selbst. Stets legen sie jedoch einen besonderen Charme an den Tag und sind harmonisch in die architektonische Hülle eingepasst. Es sind Heimstätten voller Kunstwerke, Antiquitäten, Sammlerstücke, Altes vermischt sich mit Neuem, Designermöbel setzen Akzente in Räumen mit sehr klarer Linienführung und die Auswahl der Materialien und Farben zeugt von Fachwissen und Sorgfalt.

Geschickt werden Wohnungen über zwei Etagen zusammengelegt, um den Wohnraum zu vergrößern und Trennwände errichtet oder herausgerissen, um den Grundriss den individuellen Bedürfnissen anzupassen. Ein Arbeitsplatz mit Computer findet in einer Nische Platz und Einbaumöbel schaffen den nötigen Stauraum, ohne das Auge zu provozieren. Ein offener Kamin kann Reminiszenz an die gesellschaftlichen Gepflogenheiten vergangener Epochen sein oder in moderner Form als dekoratives Heizelement die Atmosphäre im Wohnzimmer im doppelten Sinne erwärmen. Alte freigelegte Dachbalken brechen mit der Kühle einer von Weiß dominierten Einrichtung und über Jahre gewachsene Stillleben von Kunstwerken und Sammlerstücken beleben unsere Neugier, mehr über den Bewohner und sein Leben zu erfahren. Jedes der vorgestellten Häuser ist ebenso wie die Wohnungen und Apartments eine Oase des Intimen gegenüber dem Trubel, dem „grande casino", das sich allgegenwärtig auf den Straßen und Plätzen abspielt.

Die Herausgeberinnen dieses Buches möchten allen Beteiligten ihren Dank aussprechen, uns diesen vertrauensvollen Blick hinter die Kulissen werfen zu lassen. Und nach der letzten Seite spätestens steht der Entschluss fest: Beim nächsten Besuch in der ewigen Stadt werden solange Münzen in den Trevi-Brunnen geworfen, bis auch wir in den Genuss eines **Rome Houses** kommen.

Presentazione

Roma – sono solo poche lettere, ma basta sentirne il suono per sprofondare immediatamente in un silenzio solenne e abbandonarsi a sogni ad occhi aperti e magari anche a ricordi trasfigurati. Questa città emana un fascino come pochi altri posti al mondo.

Roma – la città bella, eterna, aperta... Quanti aggettivi la possono descrivere? Teatro millenario di una storia commuovente, di cultura raffinata e tesori d'arte, ma anche di ricchezza d'ingegno e dinamismo. Davanti al nostro occhio interiore affiorano pietre, pietre molto antiche e un groviglio di strade larghe che portano sui colli e poi viuzze, calca e traffico che toglie il respiro. Il profumo del cappuccino fa da sfondo a una sfilata di persone eleganti, a onnipresenti gruppi di turisti e a passanti solitari assetati di conoscenza. Profili romani marcati, capelli lucenti e occhiali da sole di giorno e di notte. L'immagine è colorata e turbolenta, piena di gioia di vivere e ricca di gestualità. Spezzoni di film si mescolano con idilli da cartolina, mentre disegni tratti da libri di storia si confondono con ricordi di visite ai musei e immagini televisive dell'ultima benedizione papale.

Infinite sono le chiese, le vie e gli angoli; il visitatore può abbandonarsi senza riserve a questa vita animata, ma ciò che ci emoziona maggiormente sono i monumenti famosi in tutto il mondo: il Vaticano con la Chiesa di San Pietro, il Colosseo, il Foro Romano, il Mausoleo, la scalinata di Piazza di Spagna, il Pantheon, solo per citarne alcuni, senza dimenticare – bisogna lasciare che il nome si sciolga sulla lingua come un gelato cremoso alla stracciatella oppure pronunciarlo con l'ardore con cui Kevin Kline nel film "Un pesce di nome Wanda" cercava di convincere la sua partner – la Fontana di Trevi...

Negozi curiosi, boutique di moda, ristoranti, bar, caffè: sono molti i diversivi rispetto ai musei e ai tesori d'arte – soltanto la noia è estranea alla capitale d'Italia. Ciò nonostante, questo libro non parla del volto noto della città, al contrario – i lettori possono guardare direttamente nelle stanze private dei romani invece che farlo dalla finestra di una camera d'hotel o dall'autobus. Antiche porte si aprono scricchiolando, i giardini pensili, dei quali si intuisce la presenza dalla

strada, invitano ad indugiare voluttuosamente sui sette colli, e gli utensili da cucina dalla lucida cromatura danno finalmente un senso alle migliaia di specialità che si possono acquistare nei mercati ben forniti.

I romani non sanno rinunciare alla bellezza della loro città. Nelle ville, nelle case e negli appartamenti privati, il visitatore viene accolto dagli stili e dalle atmosfere più diverse create da architetti, progettisti d'interni o inquilini esperti di design; gli ambienti mostrano uno charme del tutto particolare e sono integrati armonicamente nella cornice architettonica. Si tratta di abitazioni piene di opere d'arte, oggetti d'antiquariato e pezzi da collezione, dove l'antico si mescola con il moderno e mobili di design spiccano in spazi delineati molto chiaramente, mentre la scelta dei materiali e dei colori testimonia sapienza e attenzione estreme.

Si uniscono appartamenti su due piani per ampliare in modo raffinato lo spazio abitativo, si installano o si eliminano pareti divisorie per adattare la struttura alle esigenze individuali. In una nicchia trova posto un tavolo da lavoro con computer, mentre mobili incassati creano lo spazio necessario senza stonature. Un camino aperto può ricordare i riti mondani di epoche passate o, in forma moderna, scaldare l'atmosfera del salotto anche come elemento decorativo. Le antiche travi del soffitto spezzano la freddezza di un arredamento dominato dal bianco, e nature morte composte da opere d'arte e pezzi da collezione che aumentano con il passare del tempo risvegliano la nostra curiosità di conoscere meglio l'inquilino e la sua vita. Ognuna delle case e degli appartamenti presentati è un'oasi di intimità in contrasto con la confusione, il "grande casino" onnipresente nelle strade e nelle piazze.

Le curatrici di questo libro ringraziano tutte le persone coinvolte per averci permesso di lanciare uno sguardo fiducioso dietro le quinte. E arrivati all'ultima pagina, ci rimane un proposito da soddisfare: nella prossima visita alla città eterna, lanceremo monetine nella Fontana di Trevi finché anche noi non proveremo il piacere di entrare in una delle **Rome Houses**.

Introducción

Roma. El simple sonido de esas cuatro letras induce absortos silencios soñadores que incluso pueden avivar recuerdos amarilleados por el tiempo. Una ciudad fascinante como pocos lugares en el mundo.

Roma, ciudad hermosa, eterna, abierta... ¿Cuántos adjetivos podríamos añadir? Durante milenios ha sido escenario del devenir de la historia, de la cultura más excelsa, de tesoros artísticos, de la imaginación y el dinamismo. Restos de la antiguedad, amplias avenidas y un laberinto de callejones que serpentean por las colinas que albergan la multitud y el tráfico vertiginoso. El aroma de capuccino recién hecho como fondo para un desfile de gente elegantemente vestida entre la cual se encuentran turistas por doquier, en grupos o solitarios sedientos de cultura. Marcados perfiles romanos, cabellos brillantes y gafas de sol tanto de día como de noche. El cuadro es colorista, turbulento y vital, animado por expresivos gestos de rostros y manos. Escenas de película se mezclan con idilios de postal; las ilustraciones de los libros de historia, con recuerdos de visitas a museos e imágenes televisivas de la última bendición papal.

En sus incontables iglesias, callejones y rincones, el visitante puede simplemente dejarse llevar por el bullicioso día a día, pero son sin duda los mundialmente conocidos monumentos de Roma los que nos causan palpitaciones: el Vaticano con la catedral de San Pedro, el Coliseo, el Foro Romano, el Mausoleo, la plaza de España, el Panteón y la Fontana di Trevi –y dejemos que este último nombre se diluya en la lengua como un helado de stracciatella, o pronunciémoslo con tanto ardor como Kevin Kline ponía en encender la pasión de su pareja en "Un pez llamado Wanda"–.

Curiosos negocios, boutiques de moda, restaurantes, bares y cafés... En Roma, las posibilidades de distraerse fuera de museos y otros tesoros artísticos son grandes. Resulta difícil aburrirse en la capital de Italia. Pero este libro no aborda este rostro de la ciudad, el más conocido. Bien al contrario, el lector dejará de observar desde la ventana del hotel o del autobús para dirigir su mirada a los más privados espacios de la Roma de hoy en día. Antiguas puertas que se abren con un chirrido, jardines en azoteas apenas perceptibles desde la calle que invitan a reco-

rrer placenteramente con la vista las siete colinas, cocinas adornadas con preciosos utensilios cromados dispuestos a preparar las muchas especialidades que se ofrecen en los abundantes mercados romanos.

Los romanos no pueden resistirse a la belleza de su ciudad. En las villas privadas, en las casas y los pisos, los estilos y las atmósferas más diferentes salen al encuentro del visitante. Diseñados por arquitectos, interioristas o los mismos inquilinos con afición por la decoración, dejan patente un encanto especial y una armoniosa adaptación a la estructura arquitectónica. Lo viejo convive con lo nuevo en hogares familiares repletos de obras de arte, antigüedades, piezas de coleccionismo, muebles de diseño que otorgan carácter a estancias de líneas simples y limpias, donde la elección de los materiales atestigua cuidado y saber hacer.

Viviendas de dos plantas se comunican habilidosamente para ampliar el salón, y paredes divisorias se levantan o se eliminan para adaptar la construcción a las necesidades individuales de la mejor forma posible. La mesa para trabajar con el ordenador encuentra su espacio en un hueco de la pared, y un mueble modular permite disfrutar de un trastero tan discreto como indispensable. Una chimenea abierta puede ser una reminiscencia de las costumbres de sociedad de una época o, en su versión moderna, templar el ambiente, en un doble sentido de la expresión. Antiguas vigas al descubierto rompen con la frialdad de una decoración dominada por el blanco, y bodegones de obras de arte y piezas de coleccionismo acumulados durante años despiertan nuestra curiosidad por saber más sobre el inquilino y su vida. Cada una de las casas presentadas, cada piso o apartamento, es un oasis frente al tumulto, el "grande casino", que domina calles y plazas.

Las editoras de este libro agradecen desde estas líneas a todos los que en él han colaborado el habernos permitido echar esta confidente mirada tras los escenarios. Y esperan que cuando el lector llegue a la última página, si no antes, tome una determinación: en su próxima visita a la ciudad eterna lanzará monedas a la Fontana di Trevi hasta que también pueda disfrutar del placer de una **casa en Roma**.

Laura Biagiotti

Laura Biagiotti

Fashion designer and art aficionado Laura Biagiotti renovated this former **medieval fortress** over a period of five years under the watchful eye of Italy's Istituto delle Belle Arti (Academy of fine art), and the castle now serves as Biagiotti's residence and corporate headquarters. Its magnificent frescoes are from the Renaissance and Baroque eras. The incredible atmosphere of this "living museum" gives one the uncanny feeling of being back in medieval times. This enchanting ambience is palpable as soon as you walk through the portal into the light-flooded inner courtyard.

Dieses **mittelalterliche Schloss** wurde jahrelangen Renovierungsarbeiten unter dem achtsamen Auge des Istituto delle Belle Arti, Italiens Institut der schönen Künste unterzogen. Die enthusiastische Kunstliebhaberin und Designerin Laura Biagiotti lebt und arbeitet in diesem einzigartigen altertümlichen Gemäuer. Die sagenhaften Fresken stammen aus der Zeit zwischen der italienischen Renaissance und dem Barock. Das unglaubliche Ambiente dieses **„bewohnbaren Museums"** versetzt einen regelrecht in die Antike zurück. Schon beim Eintreten durch das Eingangsportal in das lichte Patio wird man verzaubert.

Questo **castello medievale** è stato sottoposto per anni a lavori di restauro sotto l'occhio attento dell'Istituto delle Belle Arti. L'appassionata di arte e designer Laura Biagiotti vive e lavora tra queste antiche mura così affascinanti. I favolosi affreschi risalgono al periodo tra Rinascimento italiano e Barocco. La collocazione incredibile di questo **"museo abitabile"** ci riporta a ritroso nel tempo fin nell'antichità. Basta entrare nel patio luminoso dal portone principale per restarne incantati.

Este **castillo medieval** fue sometido durante años a obras de renovación bajo la atenta mirada del Istituto delle Belle Arti, el Instituto Italiano de Bellas Artes. Laura Biagiotti, entusiasta diseñadora y aficionada al arte, vive y trabaja entre los vetustos muros de este extraordinario palacio. Sus magníficos frescos son de la época comprendida entre el renacimiento y barroco italianos. El increíble ambiente de este **"museo viviente"** te catapulta directamente al pasado. Nada más atravesar el portal y poner los pies en el patio iluminado se queda uno hechizado.

Apartment in Via Levico

Filippo Bombace

A series of novel techniques and unusual materials were used when this

dwelling was converted into a modern apartment. The **horizon-**

tal ledges that were integrated into the brownstone walls

accentuate the overall length of the apartment. In addition, a beige

color scheme contrasts pleasingly with the dark brown parquet floors

which hark back to the rustic ambiance of the original apartment. The

kitchen, which is adjacent to the living room, can be concealed behind

moveable drapes. The self-contained bedroom has

an ensuite bathroom with a large bathtub placed imposingly right in the

center of the space.

Beim Ausbau in ein modernes Apartment wurde hier eine Reihe neuer Techniken und spezielle Materialien eingesetzt. In die Mauer aus Sandstein sind **horizontale Absätze** eingearbeitet, welche die Länge der gesamten Wohnung hervorheben. Außerdem bietet ihr beiger Farbton einen schönen Kontrast zu dem tiefbraunen Holzboden, der an das rustikale Ambiente der ursprünglichen Wohnung erinnern soll. Die Küche grenzt an das Wohnzimmer und kann durch einen **automatisch verstellbaren Vorhang** kaschiert werden. Das Schlafzimmer ist eine unabhängige Suite, die mit einem Badezimmer ausgestattet ist, in dessen Mitte eine große Badewanne thront.

Durante la trasformazione di questa abitazione in un moderno appartamento, sono state impiegate tecniche e materiali innovativi. Nei muri in pietra arenaria sono state inserite **smussature orizzontali** che seguono l'appartamento in tutta la sua lunghezza; la loro tonalità di beige crea un bel contrasto con il parquet di un marrone intenso, una reminiscenza dell'ambiente rustico dell'appartamento originario. La cucina che confina con il soggiorno può venire nascosta da una **tenda regolabile automaticamente**. La camera da letto è una suite indipendente fornita di stanza da bagno, in mezzo alla quale troneggia una grande vasca.

El diseño de este nuevo apartamento se realizó aprovechando toda una serie de técnicas y materiales nuevos. En las paredes de gres se ven **huecos horizontales** que acentúan la longitud de la vivienda. Además, su color beige forma un bello contraste con los suelos de madera marrón oscuro, que pretenden rememorar el ambiente rústico de la anterior vivienda. La cocina limita con el salón, pero ambos espacios pueden separarse por una **cortina** que se corre de forma **automática**. El dormitorio es una suite independiente y posee baño propio con una gran bañera en el centro.

Pino Casagrande

Patrizio Romano Paris

This villa at the foot of Aventin Hill is the home of art collector and gallery owner Pino Casagrande. He purchased the house in 1987 and hired architect Patrizio Romano Paris to transform the first floor, basement and garden into an "inhabitable museum".

The major design challenge for Paris was that architecture had to take a back seat to art. In addition to a Norman Foster glass table and chrome Philippe Starck chairs, the house abounds with paintings, sculptures, ceramic pieces and other works of art that run the gamut from Antiquity to the avant-garde. You can gaze at photos while lying on a Mies van der Rohe sofa bed or watch avantgarde films in the gallery.

Der Kunstsammler und Galerist Pino Casagrande lebt in dieser römischen Villa am Fuße des Aventins. 1987 erwarb er Parterre, Untergeschoss und Garten und ließ es sich von dem Architekten und Studienfreund Patrizio Romano Paris als **„bewohnbares Museum"** ausbauen. Dass sich hierbei die Architektur der Kunst unterzuordnen hatte, war für Paris eine besondere Herausforderung. Neben verchromten Philippe-Starck-Stühlen und Norman Fosters Glastisch zieren etliche Kunstwerke, Keramiken und **Skulpturen** dieses Haus im Spannungsfeld von Antike und Avantgarde. Von Mies-van-der-Rohe-Liegen aus kann man Fotos betrachten und in der Galerie kann man sich Kunstfilme ansehen.

Il collezionista d'arte e gallerista Pino Casagrande vive in questa villa romana ai piedi dell'Aventino. Nel 1987 acquistò il pianterreno, il seminterrato e il giardino che affidò all'architetto e compagno di università Patrizio Romano Paris con il compito di farne un **"museo abitabile"**. La grande sfida di Paris era quella di sottomettere l'architettura alle esigenze dell'arte. Accanto alle sedie cromate di Philippe Starck e al tavolo in vetro di Norman Foster, diverse opere d'arte, ceramiche e **sculture** ornano la casa creando una tensione irrisolta tra antichità e avanguardia. È possibile ammirare delle foto seduti sulle poltrone di Mies van der Rohe oppure guardare filmati artistici nella galleria.

El coleccionista de arte y galerista Pino Casagrande vive en esta casona romana a los pies del Aventino. En 1987 compró la planta baja, el sótano y el jardín, y encargó a Patrizio Romano Paris, arquitecto y amigo de la universidad, la construcción de una **"vivienda museo"**. El hecho de que en este proyecto la arquitectura tuviese que estar al servicio del arte fue un reto especialmente atractivo. Junto a las sillas cromadas de Philippe Starck y la mesa de cristal de Norman Foster, decoran la casa otros objetos de arte, cerámicas y **esculturas** que crean un fluido diálogo entre Antigüedad y vanguardia. Desde las tumbonas de Mies van der Rohe se pueden contemplar cómodamente diversas fotos, y en la galería, proyecciones de arte.

Andrea Truglio

By the resident
Photos © Redcover / Reto Guntli

Given this relatively old apartment's vast size and cathedral ceilings, its

residents certainly cannot claim that they live in cramped quarters!

Antiques, busts and statues keep residents company in each of the

amply **proportioned rooms**, while vast numbers of

sitting areas provide a ready pretext to while away the

days. Classic wallpaper motifs and meticulously decorated works of art

make this apartment truly **picturesque**. The bedroom with

its mirror-covered portico above an antique mini-bathtub evokes one of

the Romans' favorite pastimes—thermal baths.

Über Platzmangel können sich die Bewohner dieser Altbauwohnung angesichts der Zimmerfluchten und hohen Decken wirklich nicht beklagen. Antiquitäten, Büsten und Statuen leisten einem in jedem der **großzügigen Räume** Gesellschaft und verschiedenste **Sitzgelegenheiten** laden zum Verweilen ein. Klassische Tapetenmuster und sorgsam dekorierte Kunstwerke vervollständigen das **malerische Bild**. Das Schlafzimmer erinnert mit seinem verspiegelten Portikus über der alten, schmalen Wanne an eine der Lieblingsbeschäftigungen der Römer, das traditionelle Bad in einer Therme.

Gli inquilini di questo edificio d'epoca non possono di certo lamentarsi della mancanza di spazio viste le fughe di stanze e i soffitti alti. In questi **ambienti spaziosi**, pezzi d'antiquariato, busti e statue sembrano offrire compagnia al visitatore, mentre le **poltrone e le sedie** più diverse sono un invito ad abbandonare la fretta. La tappezzeria a disegni classici e le opere d'arte decorate con attenzione completano questo **quadro così particolare**. La camera da letto e il suo portico con gli specchi sopra la vasca antica riportano alla mente una delle attività preferite dai romani, il tradizionale bagno alle terme.

Visto el número de habitaciones y la altura de los techos de este antiguo piso, sus habitantes no pueden quejarse de falta de espacio. Antigüedades, bustos y estatuas les hacen compañía en cada una de las **generosas habitaciones**, y los diferentes **asientos** desplegados por toda la casa invitan a matar el tiempo. Motivos de tapices clásicos y obras de arte decoradas con esmero completan el **pintoresco cuadro**. Con su pórtico azogado sobre la bañera antigua, el dormitorio evoca una de las ocupaciones preferidas de los romanos, el tradicional baño en las termas.

Via Appia moderna

Patrizio Romano Paris

Photos © ZAPAIMAGES / Reto Guntli

In this unremarkable looking house near Rome you encounter art in its

purest form, as well as a contemporary take on ancient Rome featuring

a collection of objects created by prominent figures on the internation-

al **art and design** scene. For example, the Norman

Foster table and Artflex chairs in the dining room, and the red Cassina

armchairs in the library have a decidedly non-Roman feel. There's noth-

ing folksy about this home, where stone, concrete, glass and ornamen-

tal lamps set the tone. A display case with ancient **Roman**

terracotta and contemporary art glass separates the living

room and game room, which is dominated by an impeccably restored

1940s billiard table.

In diesem unauffälligen Landhaus in der Umgebung von Rom empfängt einen die Kunst selbst und das antike Rom wird einem auf modernem Tablett serviert. Hier haben sich die Namen der internationalen **Design- und Kunstszene** versammelt. Der Norman-Foster-Tisch mit den Arflex-Stühlen im Esszimmer sowie die roten Cassina-Sessel in der Bibliothek sind beispielsweise auffallend unrömisch. Nichts ist hier urig, Stein, Beton, Glas und Lichtobjekte geben in diesem Haus den Ton an. Ein Glasgestell voller antiker **römischer Terrakotta-** und moderner Glasobjekte trennt den Wohnbereich vom Spielzimmer ab, das von einem perfekt restaurierten Billardtisch aus den 40er Jahren dominiert wird.

In questa casa di campagna per niente appariscente nei dintorni di Roma, l'arte fa gli onori di casa servendo la Roma antica su un vassoio moderno. Qui si incontrano i nomi più importanti **dell'arte e del design** internazionale; il tavolo di Norman Foster e le sedie Arflex nella sala da pranzo sono vistosamente "non romani", così come le poltrone rosse di Cassina della biblioteca. In questa casa dove nulla è tradizionale, la pietra, il cemento, il vetro e la luce dominano l'ambiente. Una vetrina piena **terrecotte** dell'antica **Roma** e di moderni oggetti in vetro divide la zona giorno dalla sala dei giochi, in cui troneggia da un tavolo da biliardo degli anni '40 perfettamente restaurato.

En esta discreta casa a las afueras de Roma, las visitas son recibidas por el arte en persona y la Antigüedad se sirve en bandeja de moderno diseño. En el proyecto se han unido nombres internacionales del **diseño y del arte**. La mesa de Norman Foster rodeada de sillas Arflex del comedor, así como los sillones rojos Cassina de la biblitoteca destacan precisamente por su carácter tan poco romano. Y es que aquí todo es bienvenido: la piedra, el cemento, el cristal y los elementos de iluminación le dan a esta casa mucho carácter. Una estructura acristalada repleta de objetos de **terracota** de la antigua **Roma** y otros más modernos de cristal, separa salón y comedor. Esta última estancia está dominada por una mesa de billar de la década de 1940 perfectamente restaurada.

Lazzari

By the residents
Photos © Ricardo Labougle /
Isabel Estrada

Owners Diego Lazzari and Silvia Morera are art aficionados, a fact that is clearly reflected in their decor. All of the paintings and other artworks in the apartment were created by Silvia Morera herself and harmonize impeccably with the tasteful furnishings and collector's items in the space. Ornamental ceiling plasterwork and wall decorations underscore the lovely atmosphere of this spacious apartment, endowing it with beguiling splashes of color. The building, which dates from the late 1930s, is in the Prati district near Castel St. Angelo and the Tiber.

Die Bewohner Diego Lazzari und Silvia Morera sind leidenschaftliche Kunstliebhaber und das spiegelt sich auch deutlich in der Inneneinrichtung wider. Alle **Bilder** und Kunstwerke in der ganzen Wohnung stammen von Silvia Morera selbst und gehen mit der geschmackvollen Einrichtung und Sammlerstücken Hand in Hand. **Stuckornamente an den Decken** und Wandverzierungen runden das schöne Ambiente ab und verleihen der großzügigen Wohnung charmante Farbtupfer. Das Haus entstand Ende der 30er Jahre und liegt im Stadtviertel Prati in der Nähe des Schlosses Castel St. Angelo und des Tibers.

Gli inquilini Diego Lazzari e Silvia Morera nutrono una grande passione per l'arte che si riflette chiaramente nell'arredamento. Tutti i **quadri** e gli oggetti d'arte sono opera di Silvia e si sposano perfettamente con i mobili e i pezzi da collezione dell'intera abitazione. Gli **stucchi sul soffitto** e le decorazioni alle pareti completano l'ambiente e conferiscono a questo ampio appartamento un affascinante tocco di colore. La casa, costruita alla fine degli anni '30, si trova ne quartiere Prati vicino al Castel St. Angelo e al Tevere.

Los moradores de esta casa, Diego Lazzari y Silvia Morera, son apasionados amantes del arte y ello se ve reflejado en la decoración interior. Todos los **cuadros** y objetos artísticos de la vivienda son de la propia Silvia Morera y armonizan perfectamente con la exquisita decoración y las piezas de coleccionismo. El **estuco de los techos** y la ornamentación de las paredes redondean el cuidado ambiente y dotan a la amplia vivienda de un encantador toque de color. La casa fue construida a finales de la década de 1930 en el barrio Prati, cerca del castillo de San Angelo y del río Tíber.

By the residents

Photos © Ricardo Labougle /
Isabel Estrada

The owner of this enchanting apartment takes frequent business trips to Asia and is a textile aficionado—which is why so many superb fabrics adorn the walls and elaborately worked carpets grace the floors of this apartment. The **marble-topped table**, which the owner brought back with her from the Far East, has been placed in the kitchen, and decorative **souvenirs** are scattered throughout the apartment. The configuration of the space is noteworthy for the fact that the bedroom is perched over the living room like a balcony, under the sloping roof.

Die Bewohnerin dieses zauberhaften Apartments reist beruflich häufig in den Orient und ist leidenschaftliche Liebhaberin von Textilien. Aus diesem Grund ziert eine Vielzahl feinster Stoffe die Wände und aufwändig verarbeitete Teppiche schmücken die Böden. Der **Marmortisch**, der von einer Reise in den fernen Osten mitgebracht wurde, erhielt einen Platz in der Küche. Dekorative **Mitbringsel** finden sich in der gesamten Wohnung wieder. Bemerkenswert ist die Raumaufteilung, denn das Schlafzimmer ist wie ein Balkon über dem Wohnzimmer und unter dem Schrägdach angelegt.

L'inquilina di questo affascinante appartamento viaggia spesso in Oriente per lavoro ed è un'appassionata di tessuti; per questo motivo, numerose stoffe pregiate decorano le pareti mentre tappeti molto elaborati ornano il pavimento. In cucina trova posto un **tavolo di marmo**, ricordo di un viaggio nell'Estremo Oriente. Graziosi **souvenir** sono disseminati per tutto l'appartamento. Molto interessante è la suddivisione degli spazi, con la camera da letto posta come un balcone sul soggiorno sotto il tetto spiovente.

La moradora de este encantador apartamento viaja mucho a Asia por motivos profesionales y es una apasionada de los textiles. Por esa razón, las paredes están decoradas por finas telas y tapices de exquisita elaboración. La **mesa de mármol**, venida asimismo del lejano Oriente, encontró su lugar en la cocina. Por toda la casa se encuentran decorativos **objetos traídos de los viajes**. Destaca especialmente la distribución de las habitaciones; por ejemplo, aprovechando el techo abuhardillado, se instaló el dormitorio en una especie de balcón que cuelga sobre la sala.

Iavazzo

Andrea Iavazzo
Photos © Roberto Pierucci
Collaborator: Donatella Bernabò Silorata

This approximately 1000 square foot apartment is located in the center of Rome. The owner, Andrea Iavazzo, also did the interior design and devised all the furnishings, which were made by local craftsmen in a **contemporaneous idiom** that is suitable for a today's lifestyle. Iavazzo's architecture tends to be minimalist and is a far cry from classic and Baroque Roman architecture. He uses a great deal of **wood** as well as **bold** and strident colors which are tastefully deployed throughout the space. He is also fond of creating compositions with designer lamps as a key element, the Artemide lamp on the table being one example of this.

Diese Wohnung ist ungefähr 100 m² groß und liegt im Stadtkern von Rom. Der Eigentüme Andrea Iavazzo ist gleichzeitig auch der Innenarchitekt. Er hat die gesamte Inneneinrichtung ent worfen, die schließlich von lokalen Handwerkern realisiert wurde, jedoch gemäß der **zeitgenös sischen Lebensweise** sehr modern. Sein Stil ist vorherrschend minimalistisch und weit entfern von dem traditionellen und barocken Stil der römischen Architektur. Er verwendete viel **Holz** un sehr starke, grelle Farben, die er im gesamten Haus elegant einsetzt. Er kombiniert das Mobilia auch gerne mit Designerlampen, die auf dem Tisch stehende Lampe beispielsweise ist vo Artemide.

Questo appartamento di circa 100 m² si trova nel cuore di Roma. Il proprietario Andrea Iavazz è anche l'architetto di interni; egli ha progettato in modo molto moderno tutto l'arredamento realizzato poi da artigiani locali, adattandosi alle esigenze della **vita contemporanea**. Il suo stil è principalmente minimalista, molto lontano dal tradizionale stile barocco degli edifici roman L'architetto utilizza molto **legno** e colori vivaci, integrandoli in modo elegante in tutta la casa, combina volentieri il mobilio con lampade di design; quella sul tavolo, per esempio, è d Artemide.

Este piso tiene aproximadamente 100 m² y está situado en el corazón de Roma. Su propietario Andrea Iavazzo, es también el arquitecto que efectuó la reforma del interior. Diseñó todo el mobi liario, cuya realización dejó en manos de artesanos locales, de acuerdo no obstante con un **esti lo de vida contemporáneo** moderno. Su estilo es predominantemente minimalista y está años luz del estilo barroco y tradicional de la arquitectura romana. Para restaurarlo, utilizó mucha **madera**, así como colores muy fuertes y chillones, que despliega por toda la casa con elegan cia. Además, le gusta combinar el mobiliario con lámparas de diseño, como la que se ve enci ma de la mesa, de Artemide.

Duplex with a View

StudioRAM Architetti Associati
Photos © StudioRAM

The design challenge posed by this apartment was to combine two identical spaces and at the same time devise a new room layout. The apartment extends over two levels that are stylishly linked by a sculptural staircase comprised of a metal framework and glass steps which imbue the staircase with light. A large picture frame window allows bountiful natural light into the apartment which in any case is very light thanks to its minimalist furnishings. The public living areas are downstairs and the private areas are upstairs.

Die Herausforderung bei diesem Apartment bestand darin, zwei identische Wohnungen miteinander zu verbinden und die Raumaufteilung neu zu definieren. Sie **erstreckt sich über** zwei Ebenen, die elegant mit einer skulpturalen Treppe verbunden sind. Ihr Gerüst besteht aus Metall und die einzelnen Stufen wurden aus Glas gefertigt, wodurch sie sehr leicht wirkt. Eine große Glasfassade erlaubt dem **Tageslicht** die Wohnung zu durchfluten, die durch die minimalistische Einrichtung ohnehin sehr hell wirkt. Unten befinden sich die „öffentlichen" und oben die „privaten" Bereiche.

La ristrutturazione di questo appartamento portava con sé una sfida notevole: collegare due abitazioni identiche e ridefinire da zero la suddivisione degli spazi. Ora l'appartamento **si estende su** due piani collegati da una scala scultorea, la cui struttura in metallo con gradini in vetro le conferisce una notevole leggerezza. La **luce del giorno** penetra attraverso un'ampia parete in vetro rendendo l'appartamento molto luminoso, grazie anche all'arredamento minimalista. Al piano di sotto si trovano gli ambienti "pubblici" mentre quelli "privati" sono custoditi al piano superiore.

El reto que planteaba la reforma de este apartamento era comunicar dos pisos idénticos, diferenciando al mismo tiempo la distribución espacial de cada uno. La vivienda **se extiende ahora** sobre dos alturas comunicadas entre sí por una elegante escalera que con su estructura metálica y peldaños de cristal resulta muy ligera. Una gran fachada de vidrio permite que **la luz** entre a raudales. Eso y la decoración minimalista, crean un ambiente muy diáfano. El piso inferior acoge los espacios "sociales" y el superior, las áreas más privadas de la casa.

Masciarelli

By the resident

Photos © Roberto Pierucci

Collaborator: Donatella Bernabò Silorata

This magnificent 1940s villa is located on Rome's oldest street, the Appia Antica, which dates back to 300 BC. The house's spacious garden, which also has a swimming pool, allows for relaxed meals on a lush green lawn amidst colorful flowers. The house, whose owner is an anthropologist and modern art aficionado, contains works by prominent artists and designers. Chinese artist Thing painted the trompe l'œil in the bedroom and did the decorative painting in the dining room and bedroom as well. The dining room table and chairs are by Sebastian Matta.

Diese traumhafte Villa aus den 40er Jahren befindet sich auf der Appia Antica, der älteste Straße von Rom, **die 300 v. Chr.** erbaut wurde. In dem weitläufigen Garten mit Pool kann ma beim Speisen das saftige Grün und die bunten Blumen genießen. Der Eigentümer is Anthropologe und Liebhaber moderner Kunst. Im gesamten Haus findet man Arbeiten bedeute der Künstler und Designer. Der chinesische Künstler Thing malte das **Trompe-l'œil** in Schlafzimmer sowie die Dekoration im Esszimmer und im Schlafzimmer. Der Esstisch und d Stühle sind von Sebastian Matta.

Questa villa favolosa degli anni '40 si trova sull'Appia Antica, la più vecchia via di Roma costru ta nel **300 a.C.** Nel giardino spazioso con piscina si può pranzare circondati dal verde intenso dai fiori colorati. Il proprietario è un antropologo appassionato di arte moderna; non a caso, tutta la casa si trovano lavori di artisti e designer famosi. L'artista cinese Thing ha dipinto il **trom pe-l'œil** della camera da letto e le decorazioni della camera da letto e della sala da pranzo. tavolo e le sedie sono di Sebastian Matta.

Esta increíble villa de los años 40 se encuentra en la Appia Antica, la calle más antigua de Rom que data del año **300 a. de C**. En el extenso jardín con piscina se puede disfrutar de una ap cible comida rodeado de exuberante vegetación y coloridas flores. Su propietario es antropól go y amante del arte moderno, y en toda la casa pueden encontrarse obras de artistas y dis ñadores famosos. El artista chino Thing pintó el **trompe l'œil** del dormitorio, así como la dec ración de este último y del comedor. La mesa y las sillas del comedor son de Sebastian Matt

The Ceracchi's House

Angelo Luigi Tartaglia

Photos © Eduardo D´Antona

The patterned terrazzo floors that have been used throughout this home are devoid of carpeting inserts, thus allowing their full splendor to shine forth. Indeed, these Roman mosaic-like floors are a work of art in their own right with linear patterns that playfully interconnect and lead to the various areas of the house, including its contemporary kitchen. The architect worked closely with the prominent furnishings manufacturer Boffi on the design of the kitchen whose cabinets are in cherry wood. Just off the kitchen is the dining room from which there is a lovely view of the garden, which the residents have lovingly landscaped.

Die gemusterten Terrazzoböden, die sich im ganzen Haus finden, werden nicht durch Teppiche unterbrochen und kommen so in ihrer gesamten Pracht zur Geltung. Sie wirken geradezu wie ein eigenes Kunstwerk, ähnlich den **Mosaikböden** im alten Rom. Spielerisch verbinden sie durch ihre Linien die einzelnen Wohnbereiche miteinander und führen unter anderem in die moderne Küche. Diese entstand in enger Zusammenarbeit des Architekten mit dem bekannten Hersteller „Boffi" und besteht aus Kirschholzschränken. Direkt neben der **Küche** befindet sich das Esszimmer, von dem aus man eine herrliche Sicht auf den Garten hat, welchen die Bewohner liebevoll bepflanzt haben.

I pavimenti decorati alla veneziana, presenti in tutta la casa, non sono coperti da alcun tappeto risaltando in tutto il loro splendore. L'effetto è quello di un'opera d'arte a sé, come i **mosaici** dell'antica Roma. Le linee dei loro disegni collegano giocosamente i diversi settori abitativi; tra di essi, spicca la moderna cucina, nata da una stretta collaborazione con il famoso produttore "Boffi" e composta da armadietti in ciliegio. Subito accanto alla **cucina** si trova la sala da pranzo con una vista eccezionale sul giardino, che i padroni di casa hanno amorevolmente curato.

El suelo de terrazo con motivos ornamentales que se extiende por toda la casa no queda oculto por alfombras. De esta forma puede lucir en todo su esplendor, como si fuera una obra de arte en sí mismo como sucedía con los **mosaicos** romanos clásicos. Sus caprichosas líneas unen los diversos espacios y sirven para integrar asimismo la moderna **cocina**, creada en estrecha colaboración del arquitecto con el conocido fabricante Boffi. En ella destacan los armarios de cerezo. Al lado se encuentra el comedor desde el que se disfruta de una encantadora vista al jardín, primorosamente cuidado por los propietarios.

Apartment in Marco Simone

Filippo Bombace

Photos © Luigi Filetici

This apartment extends over three levels. The ground floor contains the entryway, the kitchen and the dining room while the bedroom and living room are on the upper floors. The entryway is stylishly concealed from the rest of the apartment by a moveable drape. Directly adjacent to the entryway is an area in which artworks are displayed on a gravelly soil. The kitchen is ornamented with a light blue pane of opaque glass. A rotatable TV on the ceiling allows for comfortable viewing from every angle. The entire living area has stone floors, while the staircase is made of coconut wood and the bedroom floor is maple.

Diese Wohnung erstreckt sich über drei Stockwerke. Im Erdgeschoss befinden sich der Eingang die Küche sowie das Esszimmer, während Wohn- und Schlafzimmer in den anderen beide Etagen liegen. **Der Eingangsbereich** ist Dank beweglicher Leinwände geschickt vom Rest abge teilt. Direkt daneben stellt ein dekorativer Bereich mit Kiesboden Kunstwerke aus. Eine hellblau Milchglasscheibe ziert die Küche und ein **drehbarer Fernseher** an der Decke erlaubt es, be quem von rings herum fernzusehen. Der gesamte Wohnbereich ist mit Steinböden ausgeleg während die Treppe aus Kokosholz besteht und die Schlafquartiere aus Ahorn.

Questo appartamento si estende su tre piani: al piano terra sono collocate l'ingresso, la cucin e la sala da pranzo, mentre il salotto e le camere da letto occupano gli altri due piani. Alcu pannelli movibili separano **l'ingresso** dal resto dell'abitazione. Subito accanto, alcune oper d'arte trovano una degna collocazione in uno spazio decorativo con pavimento in ghiaia. Un lastra in vetro opalino azzurro decora la cucina mentre il **televisore girevole** sul soffitto perme te di guardare la televisione da qualsiasi punto. Tutta la pavimentazione della zona giorno è i pietra, mentre le scale sono in legno di cocco e la zona notte in acero.

Esta vivienda se extiende sobre tres pisos diferentes. En la planta baja se encuentran la entra da, la cocina y el comedor; el salón y los dormitorios ocupan los dos niveles superiores. **El rec bidor** queda ingeniosamente separado de las otras estancias con ayuda de bastidores móvile El decorativo espacio contiguo, con suelo de gravilla, acoge y expone varias obras de arte. L vidrio opalino de color azul claro ornamenta la cocina y el aparato de **televisión** colocado sob una plataforma **giratoria** permite ver la tele desde cualquier ángulo. El pavimento del salón e de piedra; la escalera, por el contrario, de madera de cocotero, y el suelo de los dormitorios, d arce.

Casa Bagnera

Luca Pizzolorusso
Photos © Gianni Franchellucci &
Marinella Paolini

The main gathering place in this centrally located third-story apartment is its **spacious** living room whose airspace extends under the gable roof. An **iron and glass double-sided fireplace** designed by the architect screens off the dining area whose nineteenth century walnut table has been modernized through the addition of a steel tabletop. In the kitchen, gray Bisazza mosaic tiles of teak wood and basalt were used. The bedroom and guest room give out onto a terrace and the lavish jacuzzi on the spacious rooftop terrace is screened off by bougainvillea, lemon trees and other vegetation.

Hauptaufenthaltsort in diesem zentral gelegenen zweigeschossigen Apartment ist das **großzügige** Wohnzimmer, dessen Luftraum sich bis unter das Giebeldach erstreckt. Ein zu **zwei Seiten offener Kamin** aus Eisen und Glas, ein Entwurf des Architekten, schirmt den Essplatz ab, dessen Walnusstisch aus dem 19. Jahrhundert durch eine Stahlplatte modernisiert wurde. Für die Küche wurden graue Teakholz- und Basalt-Mosaikfliesen von Bisazza verarbeitet. Schlaf- und Gästezimmer ist eine Terrasse vorgelagert, und auf der großen Dachterrasse schirmen Bougainvillea, Zitronenbäume und andere Pflanzen den luxuriösen Whirlpool ab.

L'ambiente principale di questo appartamento su due piani situato in posizione centrale è **l'ampio soggiorno**, che arriva in alto fin sotto al tetto spiovente. **Un camino in vetro e metallo** aperto su due lati, progettato dell'architetto, delimita la zona pranzo, dove una piastra d'acciaio rende più moderno il tavolo in noce del 19° secolo. Per la cucina sono state utilizzate mattonelle grigie da mosaico di Bisazza in tek e basalto. La camera da letto e quella per gli ospiti si affacciano su una terrazza, mentre le buganvillea, i limoni e le altre piante sopra al tetto proteggono da occhi indiscreti la lussuosa vasca con idromassaggio.

La estancia principal de esta casa de dos pisos ubicada en el centro de la ciudad es el **amplio salón**, cuyo espacio se extiende hasta el tejado a dos aguas. Una **chimenea de hierro y cristal** abierta por los dos lados, diseño del arquitecto, arropa la zona del comedor, donde destaca una mesa de nogal del siglo XIX que se ha modernizado con una plancha de acero. En la cocina se han empleado azulejos de mosaico gris de Bisazza en madera de teca y basalto. Delante del dormitorio y del cuarto de invitados se extiende una terraza, y en la vasta azotea, las bugan-villas, los limoneros y otras plantas resguardan la lujosa piscina de hidromasaje.

Abate Russo

Barbara Abate Russo

Photos © Roberto Pierucci

Collaborator: Donatella Bernabò Silorata

This diminutive but charming penthouse apartment is located in Rome's picturesque Trastevere section. The resident, Barbara Abate Russo, is an artist and interior designer who specializes in natural design and bio-architecture. She decorated the apartment in accordance with the philosophy of Feng Shui. In every corner of the apartment, Russo has placed objects symbolizing water, fire, metal and wood, which correspond to the four points of the compass. The apartment is decorated with antique Chinese furnishings and furnishings designed by Barbara Abate Russo herself. The bathroom is done entirely in granite tiles and the lighting was designed by Remo Zanin. Russo calls her apartment "The hummingbird's nest".

Dieses charmante, kleine Penthouse liegt im pittoresken Stadtviertel von Trastevere. D Bewohnerin Barbara Abate Russo ist Künstlerin und Innenarchitektin zugleich, spezialisiert Naturdesign und Bio-Architektur. Sie richtete die Wohnung nach einer chinesischen Lebens ein, der **Feng-Shui-Philosophie**. In jeder Ecke der Wohnung platzierte sie Gegenstände Symbole für **Wasser, Feuer, Metall und Holz** in Übereinstimmung mit den v Himmelsrichtungen. Alte **chinesische Möbel** und von Barbara Abate Russo entworfe Einrichtungsgegenstände zieren die Wohnung. Das Badezimmer ist gänzlich aus Stein und Beleuchtung stammt von Remo Zanin. Die Bewohnerin gab der Wohnung den Namen „Das N des Kolibri".

Questo piccolo attico pieno di fascino è situato nel pittoresco quartiere di Trastevere. L'inquili Barbara Abate Russo, artista e architetto d'interni specializzata in design naturale e bioarchite tura, ha arredato l'appartamento in stile cinese, secondo la filosofia **Feng Shui.** In ogni ang della casa ha collocato degli oggetti che simboleggiano **acqua, fuoco, metallo e legno** in c rispondenza dei punti cardinali. Antichi **mobili cinesi** e oggetti d'arredo progettati personalme te da Barbara Abate Russo adornano la casa. Il bagno è interamente in pietra e l'illuminazio è di Remo Zanin. L'inquilina ha battezzato l'appartamento con il nome "Il nido del colibrì".

Este pequeño pero encantador ático, se encuentra en el pintoresco barrio del Trastevere. inquilina, Barbara Abate Russo, es artista y decoradora de interiores, especializada en dise natural y bioarquitectura. Decoró el piso de acuerdo con la filosofía china del **Feng Shui.** En ca rincón de la vivienda ha colocado objetos que simbolizan el **agua, el fuego, el metal y madera**, y corresponden a los cuatro puntos cardinales. La casa está decorada con **mueble chinos** antiguos y con objetos de decoración diseñados por la propia Barbara Abate Russo. cuarto de baño es todo de piedra y la iluminación es obra de Remo Zanin. Russo ha bautiza su hogar con el nombre de "el nido del colibrí".

Living with Art

By the owner & Osvaldo Baldini

Photos © Henry Bourne

This one of a kind apartment is a unique work of art. It is imbued with a joyfully **colorful atmosphere** that takes its cue from numerous eras, creating a felicitous mixture of African art and contemporary design and painting of the 1990s. Upon entering the apartment, at every turn you see imaginative **twentieth century** collector's items, paintings and sculptures by Ettore Sottsass, Damien Hirst and Walter Dahn. Each room is illuminated by various striking lamps and even the television is a Starck design.

Dieses originelle Apartment ist ein einziges Kunstwerk. Es ist geprägt durch ein **farbenfrohes Ambiente** aus mehreren Epochen mit einer Mischung aus afrikanischer Kunst, zeitgenössischem Design und Malerei aus den 90er Jahren. Beim Eintreten entdeckt man bei jedem Schritt fantasievolle Sammlerstücke, Gemälde und Skulpturen aus dem **20. Jahrhundert** von Ettore Sottsass, Damien Hirst oder Walter Dahn. Jeder Raum wird von verschiedenen ausgefallenen Lampen erhellt und sogar beim Fernsehen schaut man in die Röhren eines Starck-Designs.

Questo originale appartamento è un'opera d'arte unica. Nell'**ambiente dai colori vivaci**, elementi di epoche diverse si mescolano all'arte africana, al design contemporaneo e alla pittura degli anni '90. Ad ogni passo si scoprono fantasiosi pezzi da collezione, quadri e sculture del **20 secolo** di Ettore Sottsass, Damien Hirst e Walter Dahn. Ogni stanza è illuminata da lampade stravaganti e perfino la televisione è un opera di design di Starck.

Este original apartamento es en sí mismo una obra de arte. Tiene un **colorido y ecléctico ambiente** de varias épocas, resultado de la mezcla de arte africano, diseño contemporáneo y pintura de la década de 1990. Ya en la entrada se descubre la original colección de esculturas, cuadros y otras piezas del **siglo XX** de autores como Ettore Sottsass, Damien Hirst o Walter Dahn. Cada habitación está iluminada por diferentes y llamativas lámparas e incluso al ver la televisión disfrutamos del diseño de Starck.

Light Apartment

StudioRAM Architetti Associati
Photos © StudioRAM

Most of the rooms in this very light apartment have a spectacular view of a neighboring park to the south. The apartment reflects the characteristic **Roman architectural style** of the 1970s and 1980s. The original floor plan and room layout were retained, with narrow hallways leading to the various rooms. Almost all of the furnishings are in light colored wood and also serve as **room dividers**. For example, this design strategy was used to stylishly separate the kitchen from the foyer.

Diese helle Wohnung hat von den meisten Zimmern aus eine spektakuläre Aussicht auf eine angrenzenden Park in Richtung Süden. Das Apartment weist die klassische **römische Bauweise** der 70er und 80er Jahre auf. Innenaufteilung und Grundriss wurden beibehalten und die schmalen Korridore bilden einen Rundgang, der zu den einzelnen Räumen führt. Die Möbel sind fast ausschließlich aus hellem Holz und dienen auch als **Raumteiler**, so ist zum Beispiel die Küche geschickt vom Foyer und dem Wohnzimmer getrennt.

Quasi tutte le stanze in questo appartamento luminoso godono di una vista spettacolare su parco verso Sud. L'abitazione presenta la struttura tipica delle **costruzioni romane** degli an '70 e '80. Sono rimaste immutate la pianta e la suddivisione interna delle stanze, con stretti co ridoi che conducono alle singole stanze. Il mobili, quasi esclusivamente in legno chiaro, **suddividono lo spazio**, dividendo per esempio la cucina dal disimpegno e dal soggiorno.

Este luminoso apartamento, orientado hacia el sur, goza de unas vistas espectaculares a un parque vecino desde casi todas las habitaciones. La vivienda es una de las típicas **construcciones romanas** de las décadas de 1970 y 1980, en la que se respetaron la distribución interior y la planta. Los estrechos pasillos forman un corredor circular que conduce a todas las habitaciones. Los muebles son en su mayoría de madera clara y sirven también para **delimitar los diferentes espacios**, como sucede por ejemplo en la cocina, que queda separada del foyer y de la sala de forma ingeniosa.

Villa Gullia

By the resident

Photos © Redcover / Henry Wilson

Upon entering this Roman home, its natural style and attendant coziness are immediately palpable. Furnished with an elegant and profuse mixture of antiques and art, it is replete with collector's items and reams of books, all of which have been lovingly and tastefully arranged. Old manuscripts recount over two millennia of history and one can see into the library from the comfortable armchairs in the reading area.

Beim Eintreten empfängt einen der **urige Stil** und eine damit einhergehende gediegen Gemütlichkeit. Das römische Haus ist eine üppige, edle Mischung aus antiquarische **Holzmöbeln und Kunstwerken**. Sammlerstücke und viele Bücher sind im gesamten Haus vor zufinden und liebevoll arrangiert und ausgestellt. Alte Schriften erzählen über 2000 Jahr Geschichte und vom Leseplatz mit gemütlichem Sessel aus ist die Sicht offen in die Bibliothek

Entrando si viene immediatamente accolti da uno **stile molto naturale** e dal calore puro che l accompagna. Questa casa romana è un miscuglio sontuoso e nobile di mobili di **antiquariat in legno e opere d'arte**. In tutta l'abitazione si trovano pezzi da collezione e molti libri, sistema ti ed esposti con cura. Vecchi scritti raccontano 2000 anni di storia, e seduti sulla comoda pol trona da lettura si abbraccia con lo sguardo tutta la biblioteca.

Nada más franquear la entrada de esta vivienda, salta a la vista el muy **original estilo** que n deja de lado la comodidad. Esta casa romana es una mezcla noble y suntuosa de **antigüeda des de madera y obras de arte**. Por toda la casa se encuentran piezas de coleccionista numerosos libros, colocados y distribuidos con mucho gusto. Hay manuscritos antiguos que cor tienen más de 2000 años de historia y desde la sala de lectura, amueblada con cómodos buta cones, se tiene una vista de toda la biblioteca.

Villa Corsini

By the residents
Photos © Roberto Pierucci
Collaborator: Donatella Bernabò Silorata

This spacious 1800 square foot villa is located in the Olgiata section of Rome. The villa's interior design, which is reminiscent of the style of the 1970s, has been done mainly in ash and oak, as well as glass. For example, a glass wall between the kitchen and living room creates the feeling that the kitchen is fully integrated into the larger space. The bathroom is done in blue mosaic tiles and is integrated into the bedroom, likewise by means of a glass wall. The bedroom fireplace comes in handy on chilly days, and in warmer weather residents can sunbathe on the terrace.

Diese großräumige Villa misst 167 m² und liegt im Wohnviertel von Olgiata. Die Inneneinrichtung erinnert an den Stil der 70er Jahre. **Eichen- und Eschenholz** sind die vorherrschenden Baumaterialien, ebenso wie Glas. Die Küche ist beispielsweise mit einer Glaswand vom Wohnzimmer abgetrennt, scheint jedoch völlig offen **im Raum integriert** zu sein. Das Badezimmer ist mit blauen Mosaiksteinchen verkleidet und ebenfalls durch eine Glaswand mit dem Schlafzimmer vereint. Im Wohnzimmer kann man an kalten Tagen den Kamin anmachen und an warmen Tagen kann man im Patio die Sonne genießen.

In questa villa spaziosa di 167 m² situata nel quartiere residenziale dell'Olgiata, l'arredamento ricorda lo stile degli anni '70. Il legno di **quercia e di frassino** ed il vetro sono i materiali costruttivi predominanti. La cucina, per esempio, è separata dal salotto tramite una parete di vetro, ma sembra essere **completamente integrata** nello spazio. Il bagno rivestito di tessere blu di mosaico è anch'esso collegato alla camera da letto tramite una parete di vetro. Nelle giornate fredde, si può accendere il camino in soggiorno, mentre nei giorni di sole ci si può godere il sole sul patio.

Esta espaciosa villa mide 167 m² y se alza en el barrio de Olgiata. La decoración interior recuerda al estilo de los años 70. Los materiales de construcción predominantes son la madera de **roble y de fresno**, así como el cristal. Un ejemplo de ello es la cocina, separada del salón por una pared de cristal creando la sensación de que la cocina está **integrada** en el espacio mayor. El cuarto de baño está revestido de baldosines de mosaico azules y unido igualmente al dormitorio por medio de un muro de cristal. En los días fríos, en el salón se puede encender la chimenea, mientras que cuando el sol aprieta, es posible disfrutar del sol en el patio.

Small Apartment

NuMo architects
Photos © Claudio Nurzia, Andrea Palma

This small apartment is located on the airy fourth-floor heights of a

typical 1970s multifamily dwelling in the eastern section of Rome.

Several dividing walls were removed so as to create an open

atmosphere and meld the "public" and "private" areas of

the dwelling. The hierarchy of the three functional living areas—dining,

living and reading—is defined by the apartment's lighting design. Since

the residents wished to have only minimal furnish-

ings, a few pieces of furniture were designed that can be interpret-

ed in a variety of ways. Thus for example the bookcase in the office area

is transformed into a kitchen shelf around the corner.

Im Osten von Rom ist dieses kleine Apartment in luftiger Höhe des vierten Stocks angesiedelt, in einem typischen Mehrfamilienhaus aus den 70er Jahren. Es wurden einige Wände entfernt, um eine **offene Atmosphäre** herzustellen und um „öffentliche" und „private" Bereiche zusammen zuführen. Die Hierarchie der drei funktionellen Wohnbereiche Essen, Wohnen und Lesen wird durch die Beleuchtung definiert. Des Weiteren wünschten sich die Bewohner eine **minimalistische** Einrichtung. Aus diesem Grund wurden einige Möbelstücke entworfen, die unterschiedlich interpretiert werden können. Beispielsweise verwandelt sich das Bücherregal des Büros um die Ecke in ein Küchenregal.

Nella parte orientale di Roma si trova questo piccolo appartamento situato nell'arioso quarto piano di un tipico condominio degli anni '70. Per creare un **ambiente aperto** e per avvicinare le sfere del "pubblico" e del "privato" sono state eliminate alcune pareti. L'illuminazione contribuisce a definire la gerarchia dei tre settori dedicati alle occupazioni quotidiane, al cibo, alla lettura e al soggiorno. Dato che gli inquilini desideravano un **arredamento minimalista**, sono stati progettati alcuni mobili su misura che possono venire continuamente reinterpretati; la libreria dello studio nell'angolo si trasforma per esempio in una mensola da cucina.

Este pequeño apartamento en la zona este de Roma se asienta en el despejado piso cuarto de un típico edificio de la década de 1970. Se suprimieron algunos tabiques para crear una **atmósfera diáfana** y unir los espacios "públicos" y "privados" de la vivienda. La jerarquía de los tres ambientes funcionales de comedor, salón y sala de lectura se define mediante la luz. Por lo demás, los propietarios eligieron una **decoración minimalista**. Por esa razón encargaron varios muebles que se prestan a distintas interpretaciones. Por ejemplo, la librería rinconera del despacho se transforma en un aparador para la cocina.

Berarducci

Carlo Berarducci
Photos © Roberto Pierucci
Collaborator: Donatella Bernabò Silorata

This 1300 square foot apartment is in a modern building near Piazza del Popolo. The ground plan is longitudinal, with windows on both sides that let abundant light into the large, open space. The architect, Carlo Berarducci, lives in the apartment, which contains decorative objects from the 1960s and 1970s as well as contemporary pieces by emerging Roman artists such as Alessandro Gianvenuti and Marco Colazzo. The living room contains a black polyurethane Superonda couch from the 1960s, a Le Corbusier chaiselongue and brightly colored Alighiero Boetti paintings. Carlo Berarducci designed the bed and the painting above it is by Chiara.

In einem modernen Gebäude in der Nähe der Piazza del Popolo befindet sich dieses 120 m groß Apartment. Der Grundriss ist **länglich**, wobei Fenster auf beiden Seiten dem großen, offenen Raum Licht schenken. Berarducci wohnt selbst hier und verbindet Designgegenstände au den 60er und 70er Jahren mit **moderner Kunst** von jungen römischen Künstlern wie Alessandr Gianvenuti oder Marco Colazzo. So stehen das schwarze Plastiksofa „Superonda" aus den 60er und die Chaiselongue von Le Corbusier im Wohnzimmer inmitten einer bunten Sammlung de Malers Alighiero Boetti. Das Bett ist ein Originaldesign von Berarducci und die Kunst darüber ei Werk von Chiara.

In un moderno edificio nelle vicinanze di Piazza del Popolo è situato questo appartamento (120 m². La pianta si sviluppa in **lunghezza**, mentre le finestre su entrambi i lati illuminano gene rosamente il grande ambiente aperto. Berarducci vive qui, accostando oggetti di design degli an '60 e '70 alle **opere moderne** di giovani artisti romani come Alessandro Gianvenuti o Marc Colazzo. Non a caso, il sofà in plastica nero "Superonda" degli anni '60 e la chaiselongue di L Corbusier in salotto si trovano circondati dai dipinti colorati di Alighiero Boetti. Il letto è un dise gno originale di Berarducci mentre l'opera d'arte che lo sovrasta è di Chiara.

Este gran piso de 120 m² se encuentra en un edificio moderno cerca de la Piazza del Popolo. L planta es **longitudinal**, con ventanas a ambos lados que permiten la entrada de luz a raudale en el gran espacio abierto. Berarducci vive en el piso y combina objetos de diseño de la década de 1960 y 1970 con **arte moderno** de jóvenes artistas romanos como Alessandro Gianvenu o Marco Colazzo. Así, en el salón, encontramos el sofá de plástico negro "Superonda" de década de 1960 y la chaise longue de Le Corbusier junto a una colección de coloridos cuadro del pintor Alighiero Boetti. La cama es un diseño original de Berarducci y el cuadro colgado e su cabecero es una obra de Chiara.

Casa Via Sebenico

Filippo Bombace
Photos © Luigi Filetici

In renovating this stylish home, designer Giulio Gra placed great empha-

sis on retaining the architectonic features of the original appointments.

Thus, care was taken to keep **stylistic elements** such

as colorful patterned floor tiles, rustic brick walls and doors and windows

in which of course new panes of glass were installed. In the living room,

a wall of shelves shows or hides state of the art audiovisual equipment.

Numerous **works of art** adorn the walls of this dwelling,

including a pop-art portrait of Marilyn Monroe.

Bei der Umgestaltung dieser geschmackvoll eingerichteten Wohnung legte der Designer Giul
Gra großen Wert darauf, die architektonischen Merkmale der ursprünglichen Einrichtung zu erha
ten. Es wurde darauf geachtet, **stilistische Elemente** zu bewahren, wie zum Beispiel die bu
gemusterten Bodenkacheln, die rustikalen Backsteinwände sowie Türen und Fenster, in d
selbstverständlich neue Glasscheiben eingesetzt wurden. Im Wohnzimmer offenbart oder ve
steckt eine Schrankwand die modernsten audiovisuellen Technologien. Neben anderen **Kuns
werken** schmückt das Schlafzimmer die Pop-Art-Version von Marilyn Monroe.

Durante il restauro di questo appartamento arredato con gusto, il designer Giulio Gra si è preoc
cupato soprattutto di mantenere le caratteristiche architettoniche dell'arredamento originale
Sono stati conservati con cura alcuni **elementi stilistici** preesistenti come le maioliche del pav
mento, le pareti in mattoni grezzi, nonchè le porte e le finestre, fornite però di nuovi vetri. N
soggiorno, una parete di mobili componibili svela o nasconde all'occorrenza le più moderne te
nologie audiovisive. Tra le altre **opere d'arte**, spicca in camera da letto la versione Pop Art
Marilyn Monroe.

En el proyecto de esta vivienda, decorada con un gusto exquisito, el diseñador Giulio Gra cor
cedió especial importancia a mantener los rasgos arquitectónicos originales. Así se conservaro
muchos **elementos estilísticos** como, por ejemplo, los suelos de azulejos hidráulicos, las pare
des rústicas de ladrillo y las puertas y ventanas originales a las que se cambiaron las vidriera
En el salón, un armario empotrado oculta o pone de relieve la tecnología audiovisual má
moderna. Junto con otras **obras de arte**, el retrato pop art de Marilyn Monroe embellece el do
mitorio.

Casa di Campo dei Fiori

Laura Gallucci

Photos © Isidoro Genovese

Books, books and more books: this penthouse apartment looks like a well stocked library. The shelves on the walls extend all the way up to the dark exposed beams. The **bookshelves** are arrayed around the fireplace in the living room and act as a **room divider** for the apartment's mezzanine which contains an office with a large glass desk. Ideal overhead light for working is provided by **skylights** in the sloping roof, or by one of two desk lamps. The shiny metal wall covering in the bathroom creates a stark contrast with the vast amount of paper, leather and cloth used in the books.

Bücher, Bücher, Bücher – diese Dachgeschosswohnung gleicht einer gut bestückten Bibliothek. Die **Regale** ziehen sich an den Wänden hoch, bis sie an die dunklen, alten Balken der Dachkonstruktion stoßen, rahmen den Kamin im Wohnzimmer ein und fungieren als **Raumteiler** im Zwischengeschoss, wo ein Arbeitsplatz mit einem großen Glasschreibtisch eingerichtet wurde. Das perfekte Arbeitslicht kommt von oben durch das schräge **Dachfenster** oder von einer der beiden Schreibtischlampen. Einen starken Kontrast zu so viel Papier, Leder und Leinen stellt die Wandverkleidung im Badezimmer dar: glänzendes Metall.

Libri, libri, libri – questo sottotetto somiglia ad una biblioteca ben fornita. Gli **scaffali** alle pareti arrivano fino a toccare le vecchie e scure travi del soffitto, incorniciano il camino nel soggiorno e fungono da **elemento divisore** nel piano ammezzato, dove è stata creata una postazione di lavoro con una grossa scrivania in vetro. La luce perfetta per lavorare proviene dall'alto, attraverso il **lucernario inclinato**, oppure da una delle due lampade da tavolo. Una tale quantità di carta, pelle e tela fa da contrasto con il rivestimento delle pareti del bagno: metallo lucente.

Libros, libros y más libros, este ático parece una biblioteca donde no falta de nada. Las **estanterías** se extienden por las paredes hasta toparse con las viejas vigas oscuras del techo, rodean la chimenea del salón y hacen las veces de **tabique divisor** en la entreplanta, donde se ha dispuesto una zona de trabajo con un gran escritorio de cristal. La luz ideal para trabajar proviene de arriba, por donde se filtra a través de una **claraboya** inclinada, o de una de las dos lámparas del escritorio. Un fuerte contraste a tanto papel, cuero y tela lo constituye el material de revestimiento de las paredes del cuarto de baño: metal brillante.

Palazzo Borghese

Carlo Berarducci, Pietro Jovane

Photos © Pietro Jovane

This 160 square meter loft-style apartment is one of numerous attic apartments in the seventeen-century **Palazzo Borghese**, which is Rome's largest multifamily dwelling. This ultramodern, contemporary apartment is the total stylistic antithesis of the building's facade. The apartment was commissioned by Count Paolo Emilio Cavazza, a descendant of Cardinal Camillo Borghese who had the Palazzo Borghese built in 1614. A striking feature of the apartment is its staircase leading to a **glass platform** which in turn gives onto a terrace that affords a magnificent view of the historic section of Rome.

Dieser 160 m² große Loft ist eine der zahlreichen Dachwohnungen des **Palazzo Borghese**, de größten Mehrfamilienresidenz in Rom, ein Palast aus dem 17. Jahrhundert. Dieses äußers moderne, zeitgenössische Apartment bildet die absolute Antithese zur Fassade. Es wurde reali siert auf Wunsch des Grafen Paolo Emilio Cavazza, Erbe und Nachkomme des Kardinal Camille Borghese, der einst 1614 den Palast verwirklichen ließ. Bemerkenswert ist eine Treppe, über die man nach oben gelangt auf eine **Plattform aus Glas**, die wiederum auf die Terrasse führt, vor der aus man eine hervorragende Aussicht hat auf die Altstadt Roms.

Questo ampio loft di 160 m² è una delle numerose mansarde di **Palazzo Borghese**, la più gran de residenza plurifamiliare di Roma situata in un palazzo del 17° secolo. Questo appartament estremamente moderno rappresenta l'antitesi perfetta della facciata; esso fu realizzato per volon tà del conte Paolo Emilio Cavazza, erede e successore del Cardinale Camillo Borghese, che fec realizzare il Palazzo nel 1614. Di grande effetto è la scala che porta su una **piattaforma d vetro**, la quale conduce a sua volta sulla terrazza dove si gode di una vista mozzafiato sul cen tro storico di Roma.

Este loft de 160 m² es uno de los numerosos áticos que aloja el **Palazzo Borghese**, una cons trucción del siglo XVII convertida hoy en la mayor residencia multifamiliar de Roma. La vivienda extremadamente moderna, es la perfecta antítesis de la fachada. Fue concebida por encargo de conde Paolo Emilio Cavazza, descendiente y heredero del cardenal Camillo Borghese, quien a s vez mandó construir el palacio en 1614. Llama la atención la escalera que conduce a una **pla taforma de cristal**. De allí se pasa a una terraza desde la que se disfruta de una preciosa vista sobre la parte antigua de Roma.

Via Panfilo Castaldi

Angelo Luigi Tartaglia

Photos © Edoardo D'Antona

"No experimentation" might well have been the design watchword for this apartment whose decor is predominantly white and whose furnishings are classical in form. The resulting **ele-gance** is underscored by the **light-colored par-quet** floors. Only in the kitchen, which is open to the living room, were more robust black tiles used. The space in the relatively small kitchen has been used optimally, and space has even been found for a table with a corner bench. Wide, floor to ceiling blinds on the large living room and bedroom windows filter the natural light.

Keine Experimente – so könnte das Motto für diese Einrichtung lauten, in der die Farbe Weiß dominiert und Möbel und Einrichtungsgegenstände der klassischen Linie folgen. Die daraus resultierende **Eleganz** wird von dem **hellen Parkett** noch unterstrichen. Nur in der zum Wohnraum offenen Küche wurden resistentere schwarze Fliesen verlegt. Die wenigen Quadratmeter der Küche werden optimal ausgenutzt und sogar ein Essplatz mit Eckbank findet hier Platz. Überbreite und sich von Fußboden bis zur Decke erstreckende Jalousien filtern das Tageslicht, das durch die großen Fenster in Wohn- und Schlafzimmer flutet.

Nessun esperimento – questo potrebbe essere il motto per l'arredamento dominato dal bianco, in cui i mobili e gli oggetti d'arredo seguono una linea classica. **L'eleganza** che ne deriva è sottolineata anche dal **parquet chiaro**. Solo nella cucina aperta verso il resto dell'abitazione sono state messe delle piastrelle nere più resistenti. I pochi metri quadrati a disposizione della cucina sono stati sfruttati in modo ottimale, trovando spazio perfino per una zona pranzo con una panchina d'angolo. Le veneziane immense, che dal pavimento arrivano fino al soffitto, filtrano la luce del giorno che inonda la casa attraverso il soggiorno e la camera da letto.

Experimentos no, gracias– este podría ser el lema de este diseño, en el que dominan el color blanco, así como los muebles y objetos decorativos clásicos. El tono claro del **parquet** resalta la **elegancia** del conjunto. Únicamente en la cocina abierta al salón de estar se han colocado baldosas negras más resistentes. Los pocos metros cuadrados de la cocina se aprovechan de forma óptima dando cabida a un espacio para comer con un banco esquinado. Celosías de gran tamaño que se extienden desde el suelo hasta el techo filtran la luz natural que entra en el salón de estar y en dormitorio.

Titta
Photos © Roberto Pierucci
Collaborator: Donatella Bernabò Silorata

This charming penthouse apartment is located in a seventeenth century building in Rome's Trastevere section. Titta, who is an artist and lives in the apartment, did the interior design herself and each detail is associated with an event in her life. This is due to the fact that in her many trips abroad and visits to artist friends, she has amassed an impressive **collection of art objects** which are tastefully displayed in the apartment. The **ceiling**, whose beams are chestnut, is **high** enough to allow for a second level, thus making the apartment more spacious.

e hübsche Dachgeschosswohnung im Stadtviertel Trastevere befindet sich in einem Ge-
.de, das aus dem 17. Jahrhundert stammt. Es ist der Wohnsitz der Künstlerin Titta. Sie hat
die Wohnung selbst eingerichtet und jedes Detail erzählt einen Teil ihrer Geschichte, ihres
Lebens. Denn durch ihre vielen Reisen und Besuche von Künstlerfreunden hat sich eine beacht-
liche **Sammlung von Kunstobjekten** angehäuft, die ansehnlich arrangiert sind. Die Dachbalken
sind aus Kastanienholz und Dank des **hohen Dachgiebels** konnte sie die Wohnung auf zwei
Ebenen ausdehnen und Raum gewinnen.

Questo simpatico sottotetto nel quartiere di Trastevere è situato in un edificio risalente al 17°
secolo. È l'abitazione dell'artista Titta, che ha arredato personalmente l'appartamento dove ogni
dettaglio racconta un pezzo della sua storia. Grazie ai numerosi viaggi e alle visite ad amici artisti, infatti, si è venuta a creare una notevole raccolta di **oggetti d'arte**, disposti con cura. Le
travi del soffitto sono in legno di castagno e, grazie ai **frontoni alti**, è stato possibile estendere
l'appartamento su due livelli guadagnando notevole spazio.

Este coqueto ático en el barrio del Trastevere está ubicado en un edificio del siglo XVII. Es el
domicilio de la artista Titta. Ella misma decoró el piso y cada detalle está ligado directamente a
una parte de su historia, de su vida. Esto es debido a que en sus muchos viajes y visitas de ami-
gos artistas ha reunido una colección considerable de **objetos de arte** que están distribuidos
con mucha gracia por toda la vivienda. Gracias a la **altura del techo**, cuyas vigas son de cas-
taño, pudo construir un segundo nivel en el piso para así ganar más espacio.

237

Casa Anna

Mauro Baldi
Photos © Roberto Pierucci
Collaborator: Donatella Bernabò Silorata

This 2000 square foot, **floor-through** apartment is located on Borgo Pio near St. Peter's cathedral. This spacious dwelling contains two bedrooms with ensuite bathrooms and two living rooms. The architect, Mauro Baldi, designed several **lighting fixtures** for the apartment such as the ceiling lamp in the bedroom, and he also created the piece that is used on the column in the living room and elsewhere in the apartment. Classic parquet floors add a stylish touch and the dome of St. Peter's is visible through the plants on the apartment's lovely terrace.

Diese 200 m² große Wohnung befindet sich in Borgo Pio in der Nähe von St. Peter und erstre[ckt] sich über **zwei Stockwerke**. Die freizügigen Räume beherbergen zwei Schlafzimmer mit jewe[ils] einem Badezimmer, und auch der Salon breitet sich über zwei Zimmer aus. Der Architekt Mau[ro] Baldi entwarf einige **Lampen**, wie zum Beispiel die Deckenleuchte im Schlafzimmer, und au[ch] den Stuck, der unter anderem die Säule im Wohnzimmer ziert. Klassischer Parkettboden verle[iht] der Wohnung zusätzlich eine stilvolle Note und von der charmanten Terrasse hat man durch [die] Pflanzen einen schönen Blick auf die Kuppel des Doms.

Questo appartamento di 200 m² è situato a Borgo Pio, vicino a San Pietro, ed è disposto su **d[ue] piani**. Gli ambienti spaziosi ospitano due camere da letto, ognuna dotata di bagno, e il salo[ne] che si estende attraverso due stanze. L'architetto Mauro Baldi ha progettato alcune **lampad[e]** come la lampada da soffitto in camera da letto, e lo stucco che, tra le altre cose, adorna [la] colonna in salotto. Classici pavimenti in parquet conferiscono all'abitazione una nota di elega[n]za mentre dall'affascinante terrazza si gode attraverso le piante una bella vista sulla cupola [del] Duomo.

Este amplio piso de 200 m² está situado en Borgo Pio, cerca de la catedral de San Pedro, y [se] extiende a lo largo de **dos plantas**. Esta espaciosa residencia alberga dos dormitorios con s[us] respectivos baños y el salón ocupa así mismo dos habitaciones. Mauro Baldi, el arquitecto, dis[e]ñó algunas **lámparas** de la vivienda, como por ejemplo el punto de iluminación del techo [del] dormitorio, y también la pieza que, entre otras cosas, adorna la columna del salón. El suelo [de] parquet clásico aporta un toque de estilo adicional al piso y a través de las plantas de la fantá[s]tica terraza se contempla una vista preciosa de la cúpula de San Pedro.

Transformable Apartment

Carlo Berarducci
Collaborator: Luca Punzi
Photos © Roberto Pierucci

The space in this modern apartment can be reconfigured according to the resident's needs and wishes. The large open living room, which can be reduced in size or expanded as desired, connects with all other areas of the dwelling. A striking feature of the kitchen is its large black granite work surface which extends far enough beyond the countertop to be used as a kitchen table. The bedroom is adorned by a large blue wall behind the head of the bed.

Das moderne Apartment ist durch eine Serie von Schiebewänden je nach Lust und Bedarf de Bewohner verwandelbar. Der große, **offene Wohnraum** lässt sich nach Belieben eingrenzen od auch erweitern, von hier aus gelangt man in alle weiteren Bereiche. Auffallend ist die lang Arbeitsplatte in der Küche aus schwarzem Granit. Sie ragt am Ende so weit heraus, dass sie auc als **Esstisch** benutzt werden kann. Im Schlafzimmer ziert am Kopfende des Bettes eine groß blaue Wand den Raum.

Questo moderno appartamento può venire modificato secondo il gusto e le esigenze degli inqu lini grazie ad una serie di pannelli scorrevoli. L'ampio **soggiorno aperto**, collegato con tutte altre stanze, si può rimpicciolire o ingrandire a piacimento. In cucina spicca il piano di lavoro i granito nero, talmente lungo da diventare anche un **tavolo da pranzo**. In camera, l'ampia pare te blu di fronte al letto funge da elemento decorativo.

El espacio de este moderno apartamento se puede modificar a discreción gracias a una serie d tabiques corredizos. El **diáfano salón** se deja ampliar o reducir según la necesidad. Desde él s accede a las demás estancias. La cocina tiene una espectacular encimera de granito negro ta amplia que también puede utilizarse como **mesa**. En el dormitorio, la pared azul de la cabece ra de la cama da un toque marcadamente ornamental.

Rome 1

Pentastudio Architetti Associati
– Simone Cellitti, Francesco Triggiani,
Roberto Trippi
Photos © Alessandro Pariante

The ambiance in this apartment is mainly created by a handful of impressive, high-tech pieces of designer furniture. Architectonic elements such as a suspended ceiling in the living room, a curved glass-brick wall and the halogen lamps and air conditioning vents integrated into the walls and ceiling provide an ideal backdrop for the furnishings. The gray marble on the living room divider is a particularly elegant touch. A central island in the gleaming, modern kitchen is used for both cooking and eating, and some utensils are suspended from the ceiling within easy reach.

High-Tech und sehr wenige ausdrucksstarke Designermöbel bestimmen die Atmosphäre in dieser Wohnung. Die **architektonischen Elemente** wie die eingezogene Decke im Wohnzimmer, die geschwungene Wand aus Glasbausteinen und die in Wand und Decke eingelassenen Halogenstrahler und Klimaanlagenausgänge bieten den passenden Rahmen für die Einrichtung. Exklusive Eleganz verbreitet die graue Wandverkleidung aus Marmor für den Raumteiler im Wohnzimmer. In der blitzenden Küche kann in der Mitte am zentralen Block gekocht und gegessen werden, die Utensilien hängen zum Teil griffbereit von der Decke.

La **tecnologia** più moderna e pochi mobili di design ricchi d'espressività caratterizzano l'atmosfera di questo appartamento. Vari **elementi architettonici** come la controsoffittatura nel soggiorno, la parete bombata in cubetti di vetro, il faro alogeno e i bocchettoni del condizionatore incassati nel muro e nel soffitto lasciano sufficiente spazio all'arredamento. Le pareti del divisorio in soggiorno, rivestite di marmo grigio, trasmettono un'eleganza esclusiva. Nella cucina splendente si può cucinare e mangiare nel blocco centrale; parte degli utensili sono a portata di mano, appesi al soffitto.

La **alta tecnología** y muy pocos muebles de diseño, piezas que llaman la atención, definen el ambiente de este piso. Los **elementos arquitectónicos**, como el techo falso del salón, la pared curvada de ladrillo de vidrio, los focos de luz halógena que bañan la pared y el techo, así como los orificios de salida del aire acondicionado, ofrecen el marco ideal para el mobiliario. El revestimiento en mármol gris de la pared divisoria en el salón da un toque de exclusiva elegancia. En el módulo situado en el centro de la deslumbrante cocina se puede cocinar y comer, y algunos utensilios de cocina cuelgan del techo, al alcance de la mano.

Tartaglia's Home

Angelo Luigi Tartaglia
Photos © Edoardo D'Antona

This spacious, light-filled apartment has the feel of an art gallery, so skillfully displayed are the paintings and sculptures in every room. Even in the bathroom, a brightly colored fresco embellishes the upper portion of the pink tile walls. High, frosted-glass doors punctuated by transparent areas create a stylish accent in the entryway. Chrome predominates in the roomy eat-in kitchen—for example, in the open shelving and the various kitchen utensils, which are within easy reach. Abundant air and light stream through the door, which leads onto a balcony that is surrounded by a lush green area.

Diese großzügige, helle Wohnung erinnert an eine **Kunstgalerie**, so auffallend gut platziert sind die **Bilder und Skulpturen** in allen Zimmern. Sogar im Badezimmer überzieht ein buntes Freskenband die Wand über den pastellrosa Fliesen. Hohe Glastüren aus Mattglas mit transparenten Durchbrüchen setzen im Eingangsbereich Akzente. In der geräumigen Küche mit Essplatz beherrscht **Chrom** die Atmosphäre – als Material für die offenen Gitterregale und diverse Küchenutensilien, die griffbereit zur Verfügung stehen. Viel Licht und Luft strömt durch die Tür, die nach draußen auf den von saftigem Grün umgebenen Balkon führt.

Questo appartamento spazioso e pieno di luce sembra una **galleria d'arte**, a giudicare dell'attenzione con cui sono stati collocati **quadri e sculture** in ogni stanza. Perfino in bagno, una colorata fascia affrescata alla parete nasconde le piastrelle rosa-pastello. Nell'ingresso spiccano le grandi porte in vetro smerigliato con aperture trasparenti. Nell'ampia cucina con tavolo da pranzo predomina il **cromo** – il materiale delle mensole aperte a griglia e dei diversi utensili da cucina a portata di mano. Molta luce e aria passano attraverso la porta, che conduce all'esterno sul balcone immerso nel verde intenso.

Esta amplia y luminosa vivienda recuerda una **galería de arte**, por la perfecta colocación de los **cuadros y las esculturas** en todas las habitaciones. Incluso en el cuarto de baño un fresco cubre la pared de baldosas rosa pastel. Altas puertas de cristal opaco con detalles esmerilados otorgan carácter al área de entrada. En la amplia cocina con zona comedor el **cromo** domina la atmósfera –de este material son las estanterías metálicas abiertas y los diversos utensilios de cocina, dispuestos de forma que cuelgan para ser asidos en cualquier momento–. Abundante luz y aire entran por la puerta, que conduce hacia el balcón rodeado de un verde intenso.

Roma San Giovanni

Pentastudio Architetti Associati
Simone Cellitti, Francesco Triggiani,
Roberto Tripi
Photos © Christian Schingo

This congenial apartment has a marked classic feel about it. When it was renovated and expanded, the apartment's underlying architectonics were **harmonized** through the use of individual details that ornament the space. For example, the **column** in the living room conceals a drainpipe that could not be removed due to the constraints of the ground plan. A designer came up with this solution for the **drainpipe**, which now forms part of the apartment's decor along with the furnishings. The television is built into the wall and can be hidden from sight behind curtains.

Ein klassischer Charakter prägt dieses freundliche Apartment, das durch Renovierungsarbeite erweitert wurde. Die Grundstruktur wurde mit einzelnen Details in **Einklang** gebracht, welche d Wohnung ausschmücken. Beispielsweise verbirgt die **Säule** im Wohnzimmer ein **Abflussroh** das wegen des eingeschränkten Grundrisses nicht entfernt werden konnte. Die Idee, es so z kaschieren, stammt von einem Designer und macht nun zusammen mit den Möbeln einen Te der Inneneinrichtung aus. Der Fernseher ist in die Wand eingelassen und man kann ihn, wer man möchte, hinter Vorhängen verschwinden lassen.

Un tocco classico caratterizza questo accogliente appartamento ampliato dopo il restauro. L struttura di base è stata **armonizzata** con i particolari che decorano l'abitazione. La **colonn** nasconde per esempio un **tubo di scarico** che non è stato possibile eliminare a causa deg spazi limitati; l'idea di mimetizzare il tubo in questo modo è venuta a un designer, che l'ha inte grato a tutti gli effetti con il resto dell'arredamento. Il televisore incassato nella parete può spa rire dietro le tende.

Este acogedor apartamento, que fue ampliado en una reforma posterior, está impregnado de u marcado carácter clásico. La concepción básica **armoniza** con los detalles individuales qu decoran la vivienda. Por ejemplo, la **columna** del salón esconde los **bajantes**, que no po dían eliminarse por las limitaciones estructurales. La idea de forrarlos es de un diseñador; así s convierten, junto con los muebles, en un pilar de la decoración. El televisor, empotrad se puede ocultar asimismo tras unas cortinas.

Via Colli della Farnesina

Lazzarini Pickering Architetti
Photos © Giovanna Piemonti

The interior design of this apartment is a prime example of how Lazzarini Pickering make architecture the focus in their work and how the decor with its furniture and lamps is subordinated to the objectives of the space as a whole. The goal is to create a calm, cheery and dynamic ambiance that the residents will find enjoyable and satisfying. Rotatable elements with light gray, velvety surfaces allow the living room to be divided into various configurations and screen off the dining area with its Biedermeier furnishings. On the other side of the living room is a conservatory containing a small terrace.

Dieser Entwurf verdeutlicht sehr gut, wie Lazzarini Pickering bei der Innenraumgestaltung Architektur in den Mittelpunkt rücken und wie sich die dekorative Ausgestaltung mit Möbeln Lampen der **Raumwirkung** unterordnet. Ihr Ziel ist es, **ein ruhiges, heiteres und dynamisc** Ambiente zu schaffen, in dem die Bewohner gerne und zufrieden leben. Hier sind es **drehb** Elemente mit einer hellgrauen, samtweichen Oberfläche, die den Wohnraum flexibel aufte und vom Essbereich im Biedermeier-Stil abschirmen können. Auf der gegenüberliegenden S wurde eine kleine Terrasse in einen Wintergarten umgestaltet.

Questo progetto mostra molto chiaramente la scelta di Lazzarini Pickering di valorizzare l'ar tettura nella disposizione interna degli spazi, lasciando che la dimensione decorativa dei mc e delle luci sia subordinata all'**effetto spaziale**. Il loro obiettivo è creare ambienti **tranqu** **allegri e dinamici**, dove gli inquilini possano vivere volentieri. Elementi **girevoli** dalla superf grigio-chiara e vellutata suddividono lo spazio in modo flessibile e delimitano l'angolo da pra in stile Biedermeier. Sul lato opposto, una piccola terrazza è stata trasformata in un giardino d verno.

Este diseño es un buen exponente del protagonismo que Lazzarini Pickering otorgan a la arc tectura al decorar los interiores y de cómo la decoración con muebles y lámparas se subord al **efecto del espacio**. El objetivo es un ambiente **tranquilo, alegre y dinámico**, en el que inquilino viva a gusto y cómodo. Elementos **giratorios** de lisa superficie gris clara distribuy el espacio habitable de forma flexible y se pueden desplegar de la zona comedor en es Biedermeier. Al otro lado, una pequeña terraza se transformó en jardín de invierno.

Renzetti's Home

Raol Renzetti
Photos © Roberto Pierucci
Collaborator: Donatella Bernabò Silorata

The Roman designer Raol Renzetti often works with **wood and steel**, and this apartment is no exception. In this 600 square foot space, he combines many of his own works with objects from the 1950s and 1970s such as the living room lamp and dining room table. The steel doors are his own creation, however. This **ingeniously** designed, cozy apartment is located in Rome's historic district, Ostiense. The Pyramid of Gaius Cestius, a Roman monument that is characteristic of Ostiense, is visible through the apartment's large picture window.

Der römische Designer Raol Renzetti arbeitet viel mit **Holz und Eisen**. Er kombiniert in der 60 m großen Wohnung viele seiner eigenen Werke mit Einrichtungsgegenständen aus den 50er un 70er Jahren, wie zum Beispiel dem Esszimmertisch oder der Lampe im Wohnzimmer. Die orig nelle Eisentüre hingegen entspringt seinen kreativen Händen. Dieser **ideenreiche Winkel** befir det sich im antiken Stadtzentrum von Ostiense. Durch das große Fenster sieht man direkt auf di Pyramide des Cestius, ein charakteristisches römisches Monument dieser Gegend.

Il designer romano Raol Renzetti lavora molto con **legno e acciaio**. In questo appartamento 60 m², egli combina molti dei propri lavori con oggetti d'arredo degli anni '50 e '70, come il tavo lo in sala da pranzo e la lampada in salotto. L'originale porta in acciaio, invece, è opera della su stessa creatività. Questo angolo **ricco d'idee** si trova nell'antico centro di Ostiense e, attravers l'ampia finestra, è possibile vedere la piramide di Cestio, un monumento romano caratteristic di questa zona.

El diseñador romano Raol Renzetti trabaja mucho con **madera y acero**. En este piso de 60 m ha combinado muchas de sus obras con piezas de mobiliario de los años 50 y 70, como po ejemplo la mesa del comedor o la lámpara del salón. Las originales puertas de acero son, e cambio, producto de sus creativas manos. Este acogedor apartamento, **desbordante de ideas** está ubicado en el centro histórico de la ciudad, en Ostiense. A través del ventanal se pued contemplar la Pirámide de Cestius, un monumento romano característico de ese barrio.

Sotto le volte

Tiziana Miozzi

Photos © Tiziana Miozzi

This erstwhile abandoned 1920s villa was converted into a classically elegant modern home. The former kitchen and servant's quarters on the ground floor are now the living room. Particularly striking on this level and the one above is the impeccably restored vaulted ceiling whose decorative structural elements make for a wonderfully harmonious atmosphere. These elements were treated with a special transparent coating that protects the coloration. The colors of the floor tiles match these elements and all of the details on the facade now gleam with their original luster.

Eine verlassene mehrstöckige Landvilla aus den 1920er Jahren wurde komplett in ein modernes Heim klassischer Eleganz umgestaltet. Wo sich früher Küche und Diensträume befanden, begrüßt einen heute das Wohnzimmer im Erdgeschoss. Ins Auge fallen hier sowie im ersten Stock die sorgfältig restaurierten **Gewölbedecken**; es sind dekorative Statikelemente, die für große atmosphärische Harmonie sorgen. Sie wurden mit einem speziellen transparenten Schutzüberzug behandelt, um die unterschiedlichen Farbtöne zu bewahren. Die **Bodenfliesen** wurden darauf abgestimmt, und auch die Fassade erstrahlt mit allen Details im ursprünglichen Glanz.

Una villa di campagna abbandonata risalente agli anni '20 e costruita su più piani è stata completamente trasformata in una moderna dimora dall'eleganza classica. Dove prima c'erano la cucina e i locali di servizio, oggi ci accoglie il soggiorno al piano terra. Qui come al primo piano spiccano soprattutto i **soffitti a volta** restaurati con cura, elementi decorativi che creano una grande armonia degli ambienti; essi sono stati trattati con uno speciale rivestimento protettivo trasparente per mantenere le molteplici tonalità di colore. Le **mattonelle** del pavimento sono state scelte in base a questa varietà cromatica, e anche la facciata mostra tutto il proprio splendore in ogni singolo dettaglio.

Una apartada villa de varias plantas construida en la década de 1920 se ha transformado en una moderna casa de clásica elegancia. En la planta baja, donde antiguamente se ubicaban la cocina y habitaciones de servicio, el salón nos da la bienvenida. Llaman la atención los **techos abovedados** restaurados, elementos decorativos estáticos que confieren armonía al ambiente. Éstos han sido tratados con un recubrimiento de protección transparente, respetando así los tonos originales. Las **baldosas** del suelo son acordes a estos tonos, y también la fachada mantiene con todos sus detalles el esplendor de antaño.

Casa Bassetti

F. Bollati & E. M. Cicchetti
Photos © Gianni Franchellucci &
Marinella Paolini

Architectonic elements create design accents in this renovated apart-

ment in an older building. Immediately upon entering the space, one

notices that the concrete and steel stair-

case looks more like a well balanced sculpture than a

purely functional element. Other arresting features include the

bookshelves which extend along the walls in various

lengths, as well as wall niches that provide space for collector's

items and a bar. Rome's hilly topography is clearly visible from the apart-

ment's landscaped terrace, where a lovely swimming pool shaded by

palm trees beckons invitingly.

Architektonische Elemente setzen bewusste Akzente in dieser renovierten Altbauwohnung. Glei‹ am Eingangsbereich erscheint die ausdrucksstarke **Treppe aus Beton und Stahl** eher wie ei‹ gut ausbalancierte **Skulptur** als ein rein auf seine Funktion reduziertes Konstruktionselemer Weitere Hingucker sind die **Bücherregale**, die sich in verschiedenen Längen an den Wänd‹ erstrecken, und die **Wandnischen**, die Sammlerstücken oder der Hausbar Platz bieten. D hügelige Geographie der Stadt wird auf der Gartenterrasse deutlich, unter Palmen erstreckt si‹ hier auch ein einladender Swimming Pool.

In questo vecchio appartamento ristrutturato, gli elementi architettonici sono espressione di ur stile molto deciso. Già nell'ingresso, l'impressionante **scala in cemento e ferro** sembra più ur **scultura** ben bilanciata che un elemento costruttivo finalizzato all'uso quotidiano. Lo sguardo attirato anche dagli **scaffali** per i libri sulle pareti, di lunghezze diverse, e dalle **nicchie** nei mu che ospitano i pezzi da collezione e il bar. Dalla terrazza-giardino si delinea chiaramente la ge‹ grafia collinare della città, e sotto le palme si allunga anche un'invitante piscina.

Los elementos arquitectónicos destacan a conciencia diferentes aspectos de este piso renov‹ do de antigua construcción. Nada más entrar salta a la vista la llamativa **escalera de horm‹ gón y acero**, que parece más una escultura bien equilibrada que un elemento de construcció‹ reducido a su función original. Asimismo, llaman la atención las **estanterías** de libros, que s extienden en diferentes longitudes por las paredes, y los **huecos** en estas últimas y los divers‹ rincones de la vivienda, que cobijan piezas de coleccionismo o el mueble bar de la casa. La mo‹ tañosa geografía de la ciudad se hace patente desde la terraza ajardinada, donde además, ba‹ palmeras, destella una tentadora piscina.

Trastevere Loft

Carola Vannini
Photos © Filippo Vinardi
Art Director: Massimo Barberis

This apartment is located in the heart of Rome's titular student district

Trastevere. In renovating the apartment, architect and interior designer

Carola Vannini made playful use of modern elements and in so doing

created a space that stands in stark contrast to

the backdrop of historic Rome. In its previous incarnation, the apart-

ment had relatively high ceilings, and the architect met this challenge

by creating a space with living areas on various levels. The rooms of the

apartment are painted in different colors so as to

subtly separate the rooms and create a certain amount of perspective.

Dieses Apartment liegt im Herzen von Trastevere, dem vermeintlichen Studentenviertel Roms. Die Architektin und Innenarchitektin Carola Vannini spielte bei den Renovierungsarbeiten mit modernen Elementen und bildete somit **einen Kontrast zur** Kulisse des historisch geprägten Rom. Die Wohnung bestand einst aus einem proportional gesehen sehr hohen Raum. Die Architektin bewältigte diese Herausforderung, indem sie ihn durchstufte und Wohnfläche auf mehreren Ebenen schaffte. Die Zimmer wurden **unterschiedlich farbig** gestrichen, um eine subtile Raumtrennung zu schaffen und gewisse Perspektiven zu erzeugen.

Questo appartamento è situato nel cuore di Trastevere, considerato il quartiere studentesco di Roma. Durante i lavori di restauro, l'architetto Carola Vannini, che ha curato anche gli interni, ha giocato con elementi moderni creando **un contrasto con** lo scenario della Roma "storica". L'appartamento era composto da uno spazio in proporzione molto alto; l'architetto ha raccolto questa sfida ricavando spazi abitativi su vari livelli. Le stanze sono dipinte **con colori diversi** per suddividere in modo elegante gli ambienti e creare prospettive suggestive.

Este apartamento queda en el corazón de Trastevere, considerado el barrio de los estudiantes de Roma. La arquitecta y diseñadora de interiores Carola Vannini jugó en su remodelación con elementos modernos, **en claro contraste con** el marcado escenario histórico de fondo de la ciudad de Roma. La vivienda era en su origen un espacio desproporcionadamente alto, circunstancia que la arquitecta supo suavizar creando áreas independientes a diferentes niveles. Las habitaciones se pintaron **de colores distintos** para lograr una sutil separación espacial y marcadas perspectivas.

Revessi

Riccardo Revessi
Photos © Roberto Pierucci
Collaborator: Donatella Bernabò Silorata

This apartment is located on the fourth floor of a 1950s building in a residential area of Rome. The lightweight see-through fabrics used to decorate the room create a feeling of weightlessness. The space is done almost entirely in white, including the walls, floor and most of the furnishings. Accent colors such as gold and silver are deployed tastefully—for example in the mirror over the fireplace and the exquisite silvery Ron Arad rocking chair. The opaque fiberglass curtains just behind the fireplace that divide the room have the effect of a delicate wall. The apartment's lovely kitchen is extremely modern and practical.

Die Wohnung befindet sich in der vierten Etage eines Gebäudes aus den 50er Jahren in einer Wohngebiet von Rom. Ein offener Raum mit leichten, durchsichtigen Stoffen verleiht einem da Gefühl von **Schwerelosigkeit**. Alles ist **weiß**, von der Wand und dem Boden bis hin zum Großte des Mobiliars. Edle Farben wie **Gold und Silber** sind elegant eingesetzt, wie man am Beispie des Spiegels über dem Kamin oder des erlesenen silbernen Schaukelstuhls von Ron Arad sieh Direkt hinter dem Kamin ist der Raum durch einen halbtransparenten Glasfaservorhang getei und wirkt wie eine feine Wand. Die sagenhafte Küche ist sehr modern und zugleich funktionell

Questo appartamento è situato al quarto piano di un edificio degli anni '50 in un quartiere res denziale di Roma. Uno spazio aperto con stoffe leggere e trasparenti trasmette una sensazion di totale **assenza di gravità**. Tutto è **bianco**, dalle pareti al pavimento fino alla maggior part dei mobili. **Colori nobili** come l'oro e l'argento sono integrati in modo elegante, come dimostra no lo specchio sul camino e la raffinata sedia a dondolo d'argento di Ron Arad. Lo spazio è deli mitato da una tenda in fibra di vetro semitrasparente proprio dietro il camino, che sembra un sottile parete. La favolosa cucina è estremamente moderna e funzionale.

Este piso está ubicado en el cuarto piso de un edificio de la década de 1950, en una zona res dencial de Roma. El espacio abierto, decorado con tejidos livianos y transparentes, da la sensa cion de **ligereza**. Todo es **blanco**, desde las paredes hasta el suelo, pasando por la gran part del mobiliario. Colores de metales preciosos, como **el oro y la plata**, están distribuidos con ele gancia, como en el espejo sobre la chimenea o en la exquisita mecedora plateada de Ron Arad El espacio está dividido con una pantalla de fibra de vidrio translúcida situada justo detrás de l chimenea que hace las veces de una fina pared. La cocina es fantástica, muy moderna y fun cional al mismo tiempo.

328

Architect's Apartment

Antonio Aurigemma

Interior Design: Antonio and Marta
Aurigemma

Photos © Antonio Aurigemma

This apartment, which is located near St. Peter's cathedral, was at one time part of a larger apartment. The residents laid out and furnished the space in such a way as to allow ample room to throw parties. They also "created" an additional space by installing a **rotating wall** that opens up the bedroom, making it part of the living room, whereupon the bed simply folds up into a couch. Three objects in the apartment are tributes to **renowned architects**: one lamp is reminiscent of a piece by the celebrated Finnish architect Alvar Aalto, a concrete pillar is a tribute to Le Corbusier and the mosaic tiles hark back to the work of Gaudí.

Dieses Apartment entstand durch die Teilung einer größeren Wohnung und befindet sich in der Nähe der Peterskirche. Die Bewohner haben es so gestaltet und eingerichtet, dass genügend Platz ist, um mit mehreren Leuten Parties zu veranstalten. Sie „erfanden" einen Raum, in dem eine **drehbare Wand** das Schlafzimmer freigibt und es zum Teil des Wohnzimmers macht. Das Bett wird dabei einfach in einen Diwan verwandelt. Drei Stücke zollen großen **Meistern der Architektur** Tribut: Eine Lampe spiegelt ein Alvar-Aalto-Objekt wider, ein Betonpfeiler ist Le Corbusier gewidmet und das aus Keramikstückchen gestaltete Mosaik soll an den großen Gaudí erinnern.

Questo appartamento, nato dalla suddivisione di un'abitazione più grande, si trova nelle vicinanze di San Pietro. Gli inquilini hanno gestito gli ambienti e scelto l'arredamento in modo da lasciare spazio sufficiente per organizzare delle feste con molte persone. Essi si sono "inventati" uno spazio dove una **parete scorrevole** apre la camera da letto e la rende parte del soggiorno; il letto si trasforma così in un divano. Tre pezzi dell'arredamento rappresentano un tributo ai grandi **maestri dell'architettura**: una lampada riproduce un oggetto di Alvar Aalto, un pilastro di cemento rende omaggio a Le Corbusier e il mosaico con tasselli in ceramica rievoca il grande Gaudì.

Este apartamento es el resultado de la división de un piso más grande y está ubicado en las proximidades de la catedral de San Pedro. Sus habitantes lo han distribuido y amueblado de forma que haya sitio suficiente para organizar fiestas con muchos invitados. "Crearon" un espacio adicional colocando una **pared giratoria** que permite el acceso libre al dormitorio, de modo que éste se integra en la sala de estar. Así, la cama se convierte fácilmente en un canapé. Tres piezas rinden tributo a grandes **maestros de la arquitectura**: una lámpara evoca un objeto de Alvar Aalto, una columna de hormigón está dedicada a Le Corbusier, y el mosaico de baldosines de cerámica recuerda al gran Gaudí.

Mauro Baldi

Mauro Baldi
Photos © Roberto Pierucci
Collaborator: Donatella Bernabò Silorata

The young Italian designer Mauro Baldi designed this house and its furnishings himself. The chaiselongue in the living room is one of the lynchpins of his collection and he has dubbed it "The eye" because it apparently bears a close resemblance to an eye when folded up. The apartment's glass facade affords a lovely and relaxing view onto the landscaped terrace. Several of the furnishings in the bedroom, as well as the bookcase in the living room, are particularly striking and are above all highly practical. Nearly all of the rooms in the apartment have indirect lighting.

Mauro Baldi ist ein junger römischer Designer und entwarf das Haus wie auch einige Möbe
selbst. Die Chaiselongue im Wohnzimmer ist eines der Kernstücke seiner Sammlung und er tauf
te sie „the eye", denn wenn man sie zusammenklappt, erinnert die Form offensichtlich an ei
Auge. Von hier aus hat man durch die große **Glasfassade** einen fantastischen Blick auf die grü
bewachsene Terrasse und kann herrlich entspannen. Einige Möbelstücke im Schlafzimmer un
auch das Bücherregal im Wohnzimmer sind bemerkenswert und vor allen Dingen **praktisch**. De
Architekt setzt in fast allen Räumen eine indirekte Beleuchtung ein.

Mauro Baldi, un giovane designer romano, si è occupato personalmente della progettazione della
casa e di alcuni mobili. La chaiselongue nel soggiorno è uno dei pezzi principali della sua colle
zione; egli l'ha battezzata „the eye", perché quando è chiusa ricorda chiaramente la forma di u
occhio. Da qui, attraverso l'ampia **parete in vetro**, si gode una vista fantastica sul terrazzo pien
di piante, e ci si può completamente rilassare. Particolarmente degni di nota, ma soprattutt
molto pratici, sono alcuni mobili in camera da letto e lo scaffale dei libri in soggiorno
L'architetto ha voluto un'illuminazione indiretta quasi in ogni stanza.

El joven diseñador romano Mauro Baldi diseñó esta casa y parte de su mobiliario. La chaise lon
gue del salón es una de las piezas esenciales de su colección y la ha bautizado con el nombr
de "el ojo", porque al parecer cuando se pliega recuerda a la forma de un ojo. Desde aquí un
puede relajarse divinamente, contemplando a través de la gran **fachada de cristal** la fantásti
ca vista de la terraza ajardinada. Varias piezas del mobiliario del dormitorio, así como la estan
tería para los libros del salón son especialmente curiosas y, ante todo, **prácticas**. El arquitect
ha iluminado casi todas las habitaciones con luces indirectas.

Sami

Morq Architecture
Photos © Aliosha Merker

The living areas in this loft-like apartment which is under a slightly slop-

ing gable roof, form a single space. In the middle of the apartment, run-

ning parallel to the peak of the roof, a white partition with built-in stor-

age space and custom-made shelves, as well as an elongated concrete

bathtub, bisect the rectangular ground plan.

Two trellis-like wooden screens can be slid into position next to the bath-

tub for privacy. The craftsmanlike quality with which the decor has been

executed, as well as the use of only concrete, wood

and stucco and relatively few colors, brings out the ele-

gance of the architectonics.

Wie ein Loft ist dieses Apartment unterm leicht geneigten Giebeldach ein einziger offener Raum, in dem die verschiedenen Wohnbereiche ineinander übergehen. In der Mitte, parallel zum First, durchschneiden eine weiße Wand mit maßgefertigten Regalen und praktischem Stauraum sowie eine langgestreckte Badewanne aus Beton den **rechteckigen Grundriss**. Für mehr Privatsphäre können zwei durchbrochene Schiebeelemente aus Holz entlang der Wanne verschoben werden. Die hervorragende Verarbeitung und die Beschränkung auf wenige Materialien – **Beton, Holz, Gipsputz** – und Farben lassen die Architektur sehr elegant wirken.

Alla stregua di un loft, questo appartamento è composto da un unico ambiente aperto sotto il tetto leggermente inclinato, dove si incrociano i diversi spazi abitativi. Nel mezzo, parallelamente alla linea di colmo, un pannello bianco con scaffali su misura e un pratico sgabuzzino e una vasca da bagno in cemento dalla forma allungata tagliano a metà la **pianta rettangolare**. Per una maggiore privacy, è possibile chiudere due elementi scorrevoli in legno traforato tirandoli lungo la linea della vasca. L'eccezionale lavorazione e la scelta di limitare i colori e i materiali – **cemento, legno e intonaco di gesso** – rendono l'architettura della casa estremamente elegante.

En este apartamento situado bajo un tejado a dos ligeras vertientes, los diferentes espacios se yuxtaponen al igual que en un loft. La **planta rectangular** es dividida en su centro, paralelamente al caballete del tejado, por un tabique cortado con estanterías hechas a medida y un práctico trastero, así como por una larga bañera en cemento. Para conseguir un espacio más privado, dos paneles de madera corredizos pueden deslizarse a lo largo de la bañera. Lo arquitectónico confiere gran elegancia a este apartamento gracias a la excepcional terminación y a la utilización de pocos colores y materiales –**cemento, madera y escayola**–.

Manfredi

Barbara Abate Russo

Photos © Roberto Pierucci
Collaborator: Donatella Bernabò Silorata

This 3000 square foot house, which is located in Rome's tony Aventino section, contains ethnic art, as well as modern works by Remo Zanin and Caterina Prato Avallone. Family heirlooms such as the table are also prominent elements. The owner, Giovanna Manfredi, is the daughter of renowned Italian actor Nino Manfredi. She is extremely fond of **oriental furnishings** and art objects from China and India, from which she has also brought back colorful fabrics, including silks. Antique pieces such as Chinese crowns are on display throughout the house, including the bathroom. But the living room with its **large fireplace** is undoubtedly the heart of this dwelling.

Dieses 300 m² große Haus liegt in dem exklusiven Stadtviertel Aventino. Ethnischer Stil ist mit moderner Kunst von Remo Zanin und Caterina Prato Avallone gemischt. Aber auch alte Familienerbstücke wie beispielsweise der Tisch spielen bei der Einrichtung eine tragende Rolle. Die Eigentümerin Giovanna Manfredi ist die Tochter des berühmten italienischen Schauspieler Nino Manfredi. Sie liebt den **orientalischen Stil** und Möbel aus China und Indien, woher sie auch bunte Stoffe und Seide mitbrachte. Antike Stücke wie zum Beispiel die chinesische Kronen sind im ganzen Haus verbreitet, sogar im Badezimmer. Das Herz des Hauses bildet zweifellos das Wohnzimmer mit dem **großen Kamin**.

Questa grande casa di 300 m² si trova nell'esclusivo quartiere dell'Aventino. Lo stile etnico mescolato con l'arte moderna di Remo Zanin e Caterina Prato Avallone, ma anche i pezzi dell'eredità di famiglia come il tavolo giocano un ruolo fondamentale nella logica dell'arredamento. La proprietaria Giovanna Manfredi, figlia del famoso attore italiano Nino Manfredi, ama lo **stile orientale** e i mobili dalla Cina e dall'India, da cui ha portato come ricordo anche stoffe colorate e seta. In tutta la casa, bagno compreso, sono disseminati pezzi antichi tra cui spiccano le corone cinesi. Il salotto con il suo **grosso camino** rappresenta sicuramente il cuore della casa.

Esta casa de 300 m² está situada en el exclusivo barrio de Aventino. El estilo étnico está mezclado con el arte moderno de Remo Zanin y Caterina Prato Avallone. Reliquias de familia, como la mesa, desempeñan un papel protagonista en la decoración. Su propietaria, Giovanna Manfredi, es la hija del conocido actor italiano Nino Manfredi. Le encanta el **estilo oriental** los muebles de China e India, de donde también ha traído telas y sedas multicolores. Piezas antiguas, como las coronas chinas, decoran toda la casa, incluso el cuarto de baño. Pero el corazón de la vivienda es sin duda el salón, presidido por una **gran chimenea**.

Romano Paris

Patrizio Romano Paris
Photos © Redcover / Reto Guntli

Patrizio Romano Paris is an architect, landscape architect, boat designer, constructor and art aficionado, and this loft is a prime example of the ingenious architectural solutions he devises. The layout of the rooms creates a stage-like platform that showcases the designer furniture in the dining room as well as the overall architectonics. The inventive swimming pool located at the center of the structure is a contemporaneous throwback to ancient Roman baths. The pool is also near the middle of the livingroom, thus allowing residents to take a refreshing dip whenever the fancy strikes them.

Patrizio Romano Paris ist Architekt, Bootsbauer und Landschaftsarchitekt zugleich und außerdem großer Bewunderer konzeptueller Kunst. Bei diesem Loft beweist er sein Können mit einfallsreichen architektonischen Lösungen. Die Raumaufteilung lässt eine Art **Bühne** entstehen, auf der die Designermöbel im Esszimmer ebenso wie die Gesamtarchitektur in den Mittelpunkt der Aufmerksamkeit gerückt werden. Das originelle Schwimmbecken in der Mitte des Hauses ist sehr beeindruckend und erinnert auf moderne Weise an die alten **römischen Therme**. Es befindet sich gewissermaßen mitten im Wohnzimmer und erlaubt jederzeit eine Abkühlung.

Oltre ad essere architetto, costruttore di barche e paesaggista, Patrizio Romano Paris è anche un grosso estimatore dell'arte concettuale. In questo loft, egli dimostra tutta la propria abilità adottando le soluzioni architettoniche più ingegnose. La suddivisione degli spazi crea una sorta di **palcoscenico** che porta al centro dell'attenzione i mobili di design della sala da pranzo e l'architettura nel suo complesso. La piscina originale al centro della casa è molto suggestiva e rievoca in modo moderno le antiche **terme romane**; essa è collocata quasi al centro del salotto e garantisce refrigerio continuo.

Patrizio Romano Paris es arquitecto y arquitecto paisajista, construye botes y además es un gran admirador del arte conceptual. En este loft quedan patentes sus ingeniosas soluciones arquitectónicas. La distribución de las habitaciones crea una especie de **escenario** que llama la atención sobre el mobiliario de diseño del comedor, así como sobre la arquitectura global. La singular piscina en medio de la casa es impresionante, y es una alusión moderna a las antiguas **termas romanas**. Se encuentra, por así decirlo, en pleno salón, y permite a sus habitantes refrescarse en cualquier momento.

Apartment Viale Parioli

Carlo Berarducci, Nicola Zimatore
Collaborator: Luca Punzi
Photos © Pietro Jovane

This apartment is located in a middle-class villa that was constructed on Viale (avenue) Parioli in the 1940s. When the apartment was renovated, all partition walls were removed, thus creating a large, open

multifunctional space. A bedroom and studio

are concealed behind two sliding doors, while a 3 x 3 meter revolving door leads to the living room and dining room. In the center of the space is a wide, blue panoramic opening through which the kitchen can be seen. A striking feature of this opening is a mechanically adjustable

steel counter. When it is opened out, it can be used as

a work surface and when it is up it closes off the kitchen and dining area and serves as a mirror.

Dieses Apartment liegt in einer bürgerlichen Villa der 40er Jahre in der Allee Viale Parioli. Es sollte von allen Trennwänden befreit werden und wurde so bei der Renovierung in einen offenen, großzügigen **multifunktionalen Raum** umgestaltet. Hinter zwei Schiebetüren verbergen sich Schlafzimmer und Studio und eine 3 x 3 Meter große Drehtüre führt ins Wohn- und Esszimmer. Dort befindet sich mittig an der Esszimmerwand eine lange blaue Panoramaöffnung und erlaubt einen Blick in die Küche. Die Besonderheit dieses Fensters ist der automatisch verstellbare **Stahltresen**. Geöffnet dient er als Arbeitsfläche, geschlossen trennt er die Küche ab und zum Essbereich hin verwandelt er sich in einen Spiegel.

Questo appartamento si trova in una villa borghese degli anni '40 situata in viale Parioli. Durante il restauro sono state eliminate tutte le pareti divisorie trasformando l'appartamento in un ampio **spazio multifunzionale**. Due porte scorrevoli nascondono la camera da letto e lo studio, mentre una porta girevole di 3 x 3 metri conduce in sala da pranzo e nel salotto. Al centro si trova una lunga finestra blu che permette di lanciare uno sguardo in cucina; essa è dotata di un particolare **bancone** in acciaio regolabile automaticamente: quando è aperto diventa un piano di lavoro, mentre da chiuso separa la cucina e diventa uno specchio se visto dalla sala da pranzo.

Este apartamento se encuentra en una villa señorial de la década de 1940 de la avenida Viale Parioli. Con la remodelación se eliminaron todos los tabiques para crear un generoso **espacio abierto y multifuncional**. Dos puertas correderas ocultan la zona de dormitorio y el estudio, mientras que una puerta giratoria de 3 x 3 m conduce al salón comedor. Este espacio tiene una ventana azul alargada que permite ver la cocina. Lo especial en ella es que, abierta, se convierte en un **mostrador de acero** que sirve de encimera para trabajar y, cerrada, en un espejo que aisla el comedor de la cocina.

Casa Lo Priore

Daniela Ferragni

Photos © Gianni Franchellucci &
Marinella Paolini

This light flooded apartment on the top floor of a former **eighteenth century convent** in Rome's downtown Campo Marzio (Field of Mars) district doubles as photographer Angela Lo Priore's residence and photography studio.This apartment was remodeled by Daniela Ferragni; the living and dining areas, in which the **striking original flooring** has been retained, are the heart of this dwelling. The predominant feature in the dining area, which is furnished with a table and chairs from the 1940s and 1950s, is a painting of the last supper by Chilean-born artist Robert Sebastian Matta. Black and white portraits by Lo Priore herself are on display throughout the apartment.

Im obersten Stockwerk eines ehemaligen **Klosters aus dem 18. Jahrhundert** liegt diese licht-durchflutete Wohnung der Fotografin Angela Lo Priore im Herzen Roms auf dem ehemaligen Marsfeld (Campo Marzio). Daniela Ferragni gestaltete sie so um, dass sie sowohl als private Wohnung als auch als Fotostudio dient. Kernstück ist das Wohn- und Esszimmer, in dem der **original Fußboden** ins Auge fällt. Der Essplatz mit Tisch und Stühlen aus den 40er und 50er Jahren wird von einem Abendmahlsbild des chilenischen Malers Robert Sebastian Matta dominiert, und viele Schwarz-Weiß-Portraits der Künstlerin sind in der gesamten Wohnung aufgehängt.

All'ultimo piano di un antico **convento del 18° secolo** si trova questo appartamento luminoso della fotografa Angela Lo Priore, situato proprio nel cuore di Roma sull'antico Campo Marzio. Daniela Ferragni l'ha concepito in modo tale da renderlo sia abitazione privata che studio foto-grafico. Il nucleo dell'appartamento è la sala da pranzo con soggiorno, dove spicca il **pavimento** estremamente **originale**. Un quadro con l'Ultima Cena del pittore cileno Robert Sebastian Matta domina il tavolo da pranzo e le sedie degli anni '40 e '50, mentre in tutta l'abitazione sono appesi numerosi ritratti in bianco e nero dell'artista.

En la planta superior de un antiguo **monasterio del siglo XVIII** se sitúa esta vivienda inunda-da de luz, propiedad de la fotógrafa Angela Lo Priore, en el corazón de Roma, más concreta-mente en los antiguos Campos de Marte. Daniela Ferragni lo remodeló de manera que sirve tanto de vivienda como de oficina. Punto clave del apartamento es el salón-comedor, del cual llama la atención el **suelo original**. Un cuadro representando una eucaristía del pintor chileno Robert Sebastian Matta domina la zona comedor, con mesa y sillas de los años 40 y 50; otros muchos retratos en blanco y negro de la fotógrafa Lo Priore se encuentran repartidos por toda la vivienda.

Fendi

An original glass-and-metal construction reminiscent of an **old greenhouse** houses this elegant, light-filled home. Natural light floods in through numerous windows and is diffused through all the rooms unimpeded by dividing walls or screens. **A single space** on a rectangular plan contains the bedroom, with a majestic bed facing the exterior; and the living room. The very high pitched roof enabled the building of an attic over the entrance, and thus another sleeping zone. Both here and on the ground floor, different nooks invite one to sit down and enjoy the light-filled space and the decoration, including many paintings of animals and several sets of glass objects. This, along with the classical, rustic, and country-style furnishings, generates a setting that takes its cue from the nature around it.

Eine ganz außergewöhnliche Struktur aus Metal und Glas, die einem antiken **Wintergarten** ähnelt, beherbergt dieses elegante und lichtdurchströmte Haus. **In einem einzigen quadratischen Raum** befinden sich das Schlafzimmer mit einem edlen, nach außen orientierten Bett und das Wohnzimmer. Die besonders hohe Decke hat den Bau eines kleinen Mezzanins über den zwei Eingangstüren ermöglicht, auf dem sich eine weitere Schlafecke befindet. Sowohl hier oben wie unten laden die vielen kleinen Ecken dazu ein sich niederzusetzen, um Licht und Innenausstattung zu genießen, darunter zahlreiche Tiergemälde und verschiedene Kristallsammlungen. Zusammen mit den klassischen und rustikalen Möbelstücken schafft dies eine Atmosphäre, die unmittelbar von der alles umgebenden Natur geprägt ist.

Un'originale costruzione in metallo e cristallo che ricorda una vecchia **serra** caratterizza questa casa elegante e luminosa. In un **unico spazio** dalla pianta rettangolare si trovano la zona notte, con una camera maestosa orientata verso l'esterno, e la zona giorno. L'altissimo tetto ha permesso la costruzione di un soppalco sopra le due porte d'entrata con un'altra zona notte. Sia qui che sul piano inferiore diversi angoli invitano a sedersi e a godersi le luce e le decorazioni: diversi quadri di animali e alcuni servizi di cristalleria. Tutto ciò, insieme ai mobili in stile classico, rustico e contadino, crea un ambiente contagiato dalla naturalezza che lo circonda.

Una original construcción de metal y cristal que recuerda un antiguo **invernadero** alberga esta casa elegante y luminosa. En **un solo espacio** de planta rectangular se distribuyen el dormitorio, con una majestuosa cama orientada al exterior, y la zona de estar. El elevado techo ha posibilitado la construcción de un altillo sobre las dos puertas de entrada, con otra zona dormitorio. Tanto aquí como en la planta baja varios rincones invitan a sentarse y disfrutar de la luz y de la decoración: los múltiples cuadros de animales y varios juegos de cristalería. Ello junto con muebles de estilo clásico, rústico y campestre, consiguen una atmósfera inspirada en la naturaleza que la rodea.

Other Designpocket titles by teNeues

African Interior Design 3-8238-4563-2
Asian Interior Design 3-8238-4527-6
Avant-Garde Page Design 3-8238-4554-3
Bathroom Design 3-8238-4523-3
Beach Hotels 3-8238-4566-7
Berlin Apartments 3-8238-5596-4
Cafés & Restaurants 3-8238-5478-X
Car Design 3-8238-4561-6
Cool Hotels 3-8238-5556-5
Cool Hotels America 3-8238-4565-9
Cosmopolitan Hotels 3-8238-4546-2
Country Hotels 3-8238-5574-3
Exhibition Design 3-8238-5548-4
Furniture Design 3-8238-5575-1
Garden Design 3-8238-4524-1
Italian Interior Design 3-8238-5495-X
Kitchen Design 3-8238-4522-5
London Apartments 3-8238-5558-1
Los Angeles Houses 3-8238-5594-8
Miami Houses 3-8238-4545-4
New York Apartments 3-8238-5557-3
Office Design 3-8238-5578-6
Paris Apartments 3-8238-5571-9
Pool Design 3-8238-4531-4
Product Design 3-8238-5597-2
San Francisco Houses 3-8238-4526-8
Showrooms 3-8238-5496-8
Ski Hotels 3-8238-4543-8
Spa & Wellness Hotels 3-8238-5595-6
Sport Design 3-8238-4562-4
Staircases 3-8238-5572-7
Sydney Houses 3-8238-4525-X
Tokyo Houses 3-8238-5573-5
Tropical Houses 3-8238-4544-6

Each volume:

12.5 x 18.5 cm
400 pages
c. 400 color illustrations